בס"ד

PRACTICING SUCKS, BUT IT DOESN'T HAVE TO!

Surviving Music Lessons

Phyllis Sdoia-Satz and Barry Satz

ROWMAN & LITTLEFIELD EDUCATION
Lanham • New York • Toronto • Plymouth, UK

10 march 2
B+T
29.95(2995)

Published in the United States of America
by Rowman & Littlefield Education
A Division of Rowman & Littlefield Publishers, Inc.
A wholly owned subsidary of The Rowman & Littlefield Publishing Group, Inc.
4501 Forbes Boulevard, Suite 200, Lanham, Maryland 20706
www.rowmaneducation.com

Estover Road
Plymouth PL6 7PY
United Kingdom

Copyright © 2009 by Phyllis Sdoia-Satz and Barry Satz

Cover image and book illustrations by Gustavo Cervantes.

British Library Cataloguing in Publication Information Available

Library of Congress Cataloging-in-Publication Data
Sdoia-Satz, Phyllis, 1935–
  Practicing sucks, but it doesn't have to! : surviving music lessons / Phyllis Sdoia-Satz
and Barry Satz.
    p. cm.
  ISBN 978-1-60709-007-6 (cloth : alk. paper) — ISBN 978-1-60709-009-0 (electronic)
  1. Music—Instruction and study. I. Satz, Barry, 1931– II. Title.
  MT1.S44 2009
  781.44—dc22   2009003870

∞ ™ The paper used in this publication meets the minimum requirements of
American National Standard for Information Sciences—Permanence of Paper
for Printed Library Materials, ANSI/NISO Z39.48-1992.
Manufactured in the United States of America.

CONTENTS

FOREWORD

Practicing Sucks . . . But It Doesn't Have To! is a wonderful compendium of ideas and suggestions that provide all students, parents, and teachers with ways to make practice time fly. As both a parent and educator, I have witnessed firsthand students that lose interest in their music lessons because they didn't know what to expect, they didn't have realistic goals, and thus gave up due to frustration and irritation with the process.

Practicing Sucks gives marvelous tips about how to achieve the very best benefit from music instruction and at the same time, how to keep frustration, stress, and tension at a minimum. By the middle of the book it becomes apparent that the ideas work not just for learning music, but for learning anything. It also becomes apparent that a student who follows these suggestions diligently will advance at a pace that will amaze even the student.

There's a wealth of information in the book. Many of the ideas are wonderfully creative. Others seem very obvious (providing one thinks of them). The book talks about having the right equipment, studying in a well-lit room, having something to eat before starting to study, having realistic expectations and doable goals. There's a great section on how to efficiently memorize (and it explains different kinds of memory), how to learn material in order to retain it past the next test, how to deal with frustration so that it doesn't overwhelm the student. As a long-time teacher I can tell you that all of us have at one time or another suggested at least a few of Phyllis Sdoia-Satz's ideas to our students, but this is the first time I have seen so many creative ideas all in one place and so readily available. *Practicing Sucks* reads like a recipe book and is laid out in such a fashion that students, parents, and teachers can make immediate use of it.

Sdoia-Satz's "preludes" (little case histories that precede each chapter and point up whatever is discussed in that chapter) are true stories. They run the gamut from humor to pathos. Generally speaking, though, the authors write the material in a light-hearted manner, and it never sounds overly pedantic.

Mercy Quiroga, Ph.D.
Provost, New World School of the Arts
Miami, Florida

Dr. Quiroga is provost and chief executive officer or New World School of the Arts (NWSA) where she oversees all fiscal and operational aspects of the school, as well as the daily overall administration and artistic direction of the college and high school programs in dance, music, theater, visual arts, and other college-level instruction. Nurturing and maintaining alliances with the Florida legislature, educational partners, art leaders, and community at large to secure and maintain the school's long-term financial stability through the implementation of foundation and fundraising activities is also an integral part of Dr. Quiroga's role. Prior to this, Dr. Quiroga served as the dean of the College Division at NWSA. Prior to her role as Dean, she served as chairperson of the arts and philosophy department of Miam Dade College, Wolfson campus. Dr. Quiroga earned a bachelor of arts degree from the University of Florida, a master of arts in art history, and a Ph.D. in educational leadership from the University of Miami.

PROLOGO: PRACTICING SUCKS, BUT IT'S NECESSARY

Practicing sucks! Not many people will admit it, but it's true. Ask anyone who has ever had to practice something hundreds, perhaps thousands, of times until the body could do it absolutely correctly, automatically. That person will tell you that practicing is, at the very least, *really, really* annoying. It doesn't matter what the student is practicing . . . whether it's a gymnastic step, an ice-skating move, a tennis serve, a golf swing, or a piece on a musical instrument. The simple truth is that practicing, at best, is a boring, tedious occupation, and, what's worse, most people do it incorrectly. (Speaking of occupations, have you ever wondered why doctors "practice" but they never "perform"?)

"Wow," you're thinking. "Here's someone who finally admits to hating practice as much as I do." Oh, did you think that people who practice actually *enjoy* it? Think again! What we enjoy is the results we get from good, productive practice. And that's something that beginning-to-intermediate students *almost never do*.

Before going any further, let's first define *practice*. Practice is the monotonous repetition of one small exercise again, and again, and again, and yet again in order to teach some part of the body *to execute* it perfectly, automatically, and consistently (or to drive you crazy—whichever comes first).

Execute is a really good word to use here. By the time we train that part of the body to learn whatever it is we wanted it to learn, we really feel like killing somebody. Anybody. Maybe even the person who told us to learn it in the first place.

Nevertheless, however unpleasant it may be, if we want the brain, the hands, the feet, the fingers, the mouth, or any other part of the body to learn how to do something really well, automatically, we must practice. A lot.

THE PURPOSE OF *PRACTICING SUCKS*

I wrote this book for some very specific reasons:

- to help beginning-to-intermediate students of any instrument learn how to practice more productively and make that practice more tolerable (notice that I didn't say more *enjoyable*; when you get to the end of the book, don't write and tell me that I promised you'd learn to love practice, because that's just not going to happen);
- to enable parents of children who hate to practice to help their children become more positive and upbeat about their studies; and
- to help teachers find creative, insightful ways to alleviate the frustration that their students experience.

I have included a section for piano and keyboard students to help them optimize their practice in ways not always applicable to students of other instruments. I hope that you will pardon this seeming favoritism, but as a professional performing pianist since the age of five, I have a very personal and particular interest in wanting keyboard students to use their practice time wisely. There is also a section for vocalists, because voice is the first, the most natural, instrument.

Allow me to give you a little background about the birth of *Practicing Sucks*. As the director and owner of Sdoia-Satz Music Institute (SSMI) for forty-five years, I have watched thousands of students, from the eighteen month olds to senior citizens, pass through our doors—students of many nationalities, occupations, cultures, and musical interests. These students have had instruction in musical instruments as exotic as the Japanese koto, as weird as the nose flute, and everything in between. Some have stayed with us a few weeks, some a few months, and some several years. Regardless of the student's age, background, or instrument studied, sooner or later they all voice the same complaint: "I hate practicing. Practicing sucks" (although, admittedly, they don't all express themselves in quite those words). They grumble that it's boring, monotonous, and takes forever to learn anything. In fact, when a student terminates music lessons after only a few weeks or a few months, hating practice is very often at the top of the list of causes.

There can be many reasons that students don't get the best value from their practice and dislike it so much. Sometimes, although they try to practice, they aren't sure about how to do it; perhaps while they are practicing they're thinking about other things that they could be doing with their time; the instruments may be in poor repair; they may be studying with teachers who are not as good as they should be; they may be practicing only a couple of times each week; they may be practicing under conditions that are absolutely dreadful; and they may have little or no family support, encouragement, or interest for their endeavors. On top of that, many instructors tell students *what* corrections to make but often neglect to tell them *how* to make those corrections or why it's important, except to say "The notes are wrong" or "The rhythm is wrong; go home and practice it." Since parents can only go by what the teacher tells the student to do, they can't be of very much help, either. Because of any combination of these reasons, most students simply don't achieve as much as they should from their allotted practice time. As a result, regardless of the age of the student, frustration soon looms its ugly head, and, sooner or later, the lessons stop.

Over the years I have watched this coming and going of students repeat itself many, many times with growing frustration. I finally decided that students, parents, and teachers everywhere needed something written that gave detailed information about

- how to find a fine music teacher,
- how to obtain an instrument,
- how to practice, and
- all the other how to's that, put together, ensure success for a student who wants to learn to play a musical instrument or sing.

And so *Practicing Sucks* was born. In an attempt to keep this book from becoming too plodding and didactic, I have tried to write the important elements in a light and "chucklesome" manner. Some of the information contained in these chapters has been written by me (and probably many other instructors) in the notebooks of students hundreds, perhaps thousands, of times:

- don't play through the piece; practice in small sections, not more than a measure;
- get the instrument fixed, already; it's been three weeks;

- don't play so softly that no one can hear you;
- practice every day;
- listen to what you play as if someone else is playing it;

and so on.

All the anecdotes in the book are true. Names have been changed to protect the guilty. The information in these chapters comes from years of experience and can be read straight through or piecemeal. Each section is meant to address a particular area of concern.

It is my sincere hope that *Practicing Sucks* will be a tool that, in easy stages, once and for all, will teach students, parents of students, and teachers how to learn and practice productively, how to minimize frustration, and how to optimize the use of time, so as to derive the most pleasure, satisfaction, and inspiration that learning music has to offer.

Most of the chapters are divided into four subsections:

- for everyone,
- for parents,
- for students, and
- for instructors.

In each section, the information intended for everyone will be under *For Everyone*. Material specifically meant for students will be in *For Students*. (Incidentally, this section is specifically targeted at older students, including adults and seniors. For information for younger students, go to the *For Parents* section.)

The *For Parents* section contains specific suggestions for parents who want to help their younger child succeed in music. It is also for parents of older children when resentment, annoyance about practice, anger, and conflicts about other issues crop up.

The section marked *For Instructors* is meant to help instructors be the best that they can be. Hopefully, the tips and suggestions in the book will help instructors become more creative, more positive, more upbeat in their teaching and will cause them to discover new ways in which they can help their students attain the greatest benefit from their musical endeavors. If the ideas in *Practicing Sucks* make just one teacher, one student, or one parent rethink some of their ideas about music education, it will have done its job.

As you are reading, keep in mind that none of us ever learns anything to our satisfaction. We never learn to do anything as well as we'd like, nor do we learn it as quickly as we'd like. What's more, the more we learn, the more we discover there is so much more to know. Oh, and the old adage "practice makes perfect" is just plain nonsense. There *is* no perfection, at least not on this Earth, not for you and not for me! Nevertheless, diligent, patient, persistent, and consistent practice, using our best efforts, our highest energy levels, and the conscious commitment to simply not give up will lead the way to success well beyond what we thought we could achieve. So, go for it; the results will be worth the work!

LENTO

What You Don't Know Can Hurt You

> We are the music makers,
> And we are the dreamers of dreams,
> Wandering by lone sea-breakers,
> And sitting by desolate streams;
> World-losers and world-forsakers,
> On whom the pale moon gleams;
> Yet we are the movers and shakers
> Of the world forever, it seems.
>
> —Arthur O'Shaughnessy, "Ode"

PRELUDE

As Rebecca spoke, she punctuated her words by kicking the legs of the piano again and again and pounding on the keys with her fists. "I hate practice. I hate it. I hate it! I don't want to do it anymore! I never want to play this stupid piece ever again," she yelled.

"But I thought you liked music. I thought you liked piano. You're the one who wanted lessons," said her mother.

"I do. I like music. I do. But I hate *practice*. I hate it! Practicing sucks! I didn't know it would take this long, and I didn't know it would be this

boring, and I definitely didn't know it would be this hard. I can't learn this. I tried. I tried. I can't do it. It's just too hard," she yelled, throwing the music on the floor and punching the keyboard.

Her mother was almost as upset as her daughter. "What do you mean you tried? I never even heard you practice it."

"You don't understand. I couldn't practice it because it was too hard. That's what I've been trying to tell you. It's just too hard. This was supposed to be fun. Remember fun? Guess what, Mom. It's not fun! Read my lips: no fun! I don't want to do this anymore. Please, please call the teacher. Tell her I'm not doing this anymore."

"Hello, Ms. Pearson. This is Mrs. Sanadar. Rebecca doesn't want to continue her . . ."

FOR EVERYONE

Congratulations! Your decision to provide someone in your family (even yourself) with quality music instruction is an investment in the future. It is a source of inspiration for the student and everyone around the student. In making it possible to learn music, you are providing the opportunity for self-expression, creativity, and achievement.

Playing a musical instrument requires the simultaneous coordination of the eyes, ears, brain, hands, mouth, and, in many cases, the feet. As these skills are learned, coordination improves. Physical and mental abilities increase. Concentration and self-discipline develop. Confidence and pride overcome shyness. Other benefits include problem solving, goal setting, memory skills, self-esteem, and even teamwork. Good lessons actually teach the student how to learn faster and better. Music study also offers opportunities for shared family experiences, including:

- attending concerts and musical events,
- performing for and with family and friends,
- maybe even starting your own band, and
- learning about composers and various cultures,

all of which lead to an appreciation of music for the whole family. So much for the hype! Now for some myths and truths.

A Few Myths

Everyone starts out learning music with high hopes and expectations and way too many fantasies about how they're going to develop proficiency in a ridiculously short time. The father of a two-year-old child who can sing the notes to "Mary Had a Little Lamb" more or less on pitch thinks that with voice lessons the child can become a household name in no time at all. What nonsense!

Parents who give their shy five-year-old son violin lessons secretly hope he will be able to play at parties in a few months and thereby make friends. The teenage girl who wants to study guitar sees herself as the lead performer of the latest hip-hop band within three months of beginning instruction. Come on. Get real!

The adult beginning piano lessons as a hobby thinks she will be able to entertain friends and family within six months. What's worse, she expects to practice only about fifteen minutes at a time, a couple of days a week. Baloney!

Professional musicians (and everyone else who has been studying music for a while) know how unrealistic these expectations are. They chuckle to themselves and make bets about how long it will take before that student stops lessons. Good instructors try to tell new students the truth: that it's going to take time and it's going to take work. No one believes them! Discussing the *reality* with new students doesn't do a thing to disabuse them of their notions. They think they will become rock stars or be able to play the great masterworks of music in almost no time and with practically no effort.

A Few Truths

The fact is, in the beginning no one has a clue about how long it will take to play a musical instrument, how hard they'll have to work, or how lonely the practice is going to be. It doesn't take long, however, for them to find out—a few weeks, or at the most, a couple of months of lessons. Eventually they discover the sad truth. They say to themselves, "Wow, this is going to take a lot more than I thought it would. I don't have the time for this; I started these lessons to relax, to have fun. I didn't know I'd have to really work at it. Why should I be sitting here practicing when I could be . . ." (You can finish that statement with any of the following phrases) ". . . playing with my friends," ". . . watching TV," or ". . . doing homework."

Frustration and irritation take over. At that point, all too many students simply walk away from lessons because they didn't know at the outset how

much work they'd have to put in to reach their goals. Although it is true that some people can become musically proficient in an unusually short amount of time, the vast majority of those who learn music will need to put forth a lot of effort and spend a lot of time practicing in order to be able to play well.

Talent

This is a good time to talk about talent. What *is* talent? Talent is an ability to learn a skill well with a lot less effort and much more comfort than other people. However, even when someone does have talent, she still needs to work at it. Having talent just means that the work goes a little more quickly and is a little easier.

Many people confuse *aptitude* with *talent*. Although people often use them interchangeably, they are very different. Aptitude generally refers to potential, while talent is about skill, ability, and achievement. Talent is something that becomes apparent only after the student has been studying quite a while. Generally speaking, if the student

- almost always learns whatever the teacher gave as an assignment at the prior lesson,
- adapts pretty naturally to the strange movements the hands must learn to make automatically,
- learns to play the assignment well and fairly easily,
- consistently makes it sound exceptionally pretty and smooth,
- understands and remembers instructions made by the teacher,
- seems to eat up whatever the teacher says and makes immediate use of it,
- anticipates the teacher and begs for more work, and
- tries to go ahead of what the teacher has assigned, and is capable of it,

then it's a pretty good bet that the student has talent.

Musical Aptitude

Aptitude is something that is recognizable without much learning at all. If a person

- really likes music,
- has reasonably flexible hands,

- possesses an accurate natural sense of pitch and rhythm,
- recognizes moods and feelings of music, and
- responds to music in a positive and personal manner,

then that person is said to have a musical aptitude.

Genius

Being a genius is a whole different world. A genius at any age and in any field has a creative force that simply cannot be denied, and the talent she has outdistances anyone else's in the same field by far (unless that someone else is *also* a genius). Even the finest experts can't fathom how the output that comes from a genius develops. In the case of music, a genius doesn't just want to be a musician. Rather, she *needs* to be a musician. Emotionally, there is no choice for her, as music defines her. It isn't merely what the genius does or who the genius is. Since genius is a whole different category, and there are very few of them in the world, we'll leave its discussion to another time and another book. Now, instead, we return to aptitude and talent.

A Wonderful Hobby

There are many more people who have musical aptitude than have great talent. Talent is an unusual and wonderful gift, but people don't need a terrific talent to be able to

- enjoy music as a wonderful hobby,
- reap its therapeutic benefits, and
- derive much satisfaction and personal enjoyment from it.

Besides, sometimes aptitude develops into talent long after the student has begun lessons. The bad news is that, regardless of aptitude or talent, learning to play a musical instrument takes consistent work, dedication, perseverance, and time. Even worse, it's not like riding a bicycle; your hands *will* forget if you stop doing it.

The good news is that anything you've learned once you can relearn, and the second, third, or fourth time you learn it you will see better results faster. Think "bionic musician." Whatever you rebuild can be stronger and better than what existed originally. Musicians often relearn compositions two, three, and four times in their lives. Eventually, they understand the piece so thoroughly that it stays in their memory banks forever.

Where's the Fun?

About now, you're probably thinking, "Fine, but where's the *fun*? And if there isn't any fun, why should I do it?" There *is* fun! There is also excitement, gratification, and a wonderful sense of achievement, but all of that occurs only *after* you learn to play each piece. That's why we speak of "small successes." You don't have to learn two hours of music compositions and be able to play it in a major competition to feel a sense of joy and accomplishment. You can learn a mere thirty-second piece and find that feeling. However, getting through that one piece smoothly and easily requires work, and that work is what we call practice. Sounds tough, huh? Yes, it is, but it is *so* worth the effort. Being able to say, "Wow, look at what I can do!" gives students a terrific feeling of achievement.

Two Case Histories

Alex, a piano student at our music school, was a surgeon who spent many long hours working in a hospital. He often didn't get home before midnight and sometimes later. One day he mentioned that learning music was "wonderfully therapeutic" for him. He'd leave the hospital absolutely wired after eighteen or twenty-four hours on duty. No way could he get to sleep. When he arrived home, he'd sit down at the piano and practice intently for a couple of hours. Practice transported him to a world totally different from his everyday life. He couldn't think about anything but the music. As he focused on the need to make his fingers do what he wanted them to do, his mind began to relax. After he finished practicing, he was able to rest.

Veronica was eight years old when her father brought her to us. She was withdrawn, shy, and afraid of her own shadow (which she couldn't have seen anyway, because she was born blind). Her parents and doctors hoped that music lessons—in particular, piano lessons—would help her to develop some confidence and make her relate a little better to people and the world she couldn't see. She stayed with us for five years.

Teaching her hands to move was the easy part. Teaching her to read music was a real challenge. In order to do that, her instructor had to learn braille music symbols, a feat he accomplished in a month. Lessons for her became nothing short of a small miracle. When she discovered that music gave her a handle into the seeing world, she wanted to explore whatever else she could in that world. Gradually, her wimpy personality changed. She became much more outgoing and assertive, happier, inquisitive, and interested in everything around her, especially things musical. Eventually, she enrolled in a ballet class (yes, a blind girl learning ballet). In addition, she became part of a chorus of physically challenged teenagers that traveled around the state performing in hospitals, nursing homes, and retirement communities.

Learning by Touch and Feel

A blind person learning to play a piano isn't at all unusual. Musicians play by feel, by touch. The movement of the hands becomes automatic, and we almost never look at them, or at the instrument we are playing. We train our eyes to look in front of us at the music, instead of at the hands. An easy way to relate to this is by thinking about where you look when you're driving. You don't watch your hands, do you?

If an acoustic bass player had to bend all the way down to watch his hand moving the bow across the strings, or turn his head all the way to the side to watch his fingers on the fingerboard, it would be very difficult to play. (And think what he would have to spend in chiropractor bills.) Ice skaters don't look at their feet when they are skating, nor do skiers when they are on the slopes. Gymnasts can't watch their feet either. (Oops, that was a nasty fall.) Most of us don't watch the part of the body that is doing the work.

Practice Is Necessary

By now, you undoubtedly recognize that practice is beneficial and necessary, even if it is really annoying. The question is how to make it a little less hateful, so that students will keep at it until they have derived as much benefit from it as possible. So, let's get right to it, shall we?

FOR PARENTS

When someone studies music, members of the family must become the student's support system. While it is not the job of parents to teach or learn to play the instrument themselves, family attitude, encouragement, help, and involvement are very important factors in a student's progress. How much time and effort students put into their studies often is directly related to the amount of encouragement they receive at home. Therefore, if you want the student to appreciate the wonderful gift of music instruction that you have given, always think "positive reinforcement." Learn what you *can* do and, just as importantly, what you should *never* do in order to help the student derive the greatest benefit from her musical endeavors.

FOR STUDENTS

Learning to play a musical instrument is very much like starting out on an adventure. You are opening your eyes to a whole new world and will find out things you never even thought about before. Sometimes you'll travel the road smoothly, and sometimes the road will be rocky. The more effort and enthusiasm you put into the adventure, the more reward you will derive from it. Musically speaking, the kind of practice you do, the amount of practice, and the consistency of that practice will determine how fast you progress. There will be moments when you'll be absolutely elated. That's a good time to practice. However, practice also at those times when you are frustrated and annoyed. And when you're too tired to think, even then, practice. Whenever you have a chance, practice. You'll be glad you did!

FOR INSTRUCTORS

Instructors spend a good part of their lives learning and honing their craft. Most of us have studied for years before we ever begin to teach. By the time we've been working with students for a while, some of us feel like old hands—and maybe even a little jaded. Don't let that happen. As instructors we have the responsibility, the privilege, and the pleasure of guiding and directing the students so that they will forever consider their musical experiences something wonderful and memorable. One of the great joys of teaching is that our students not only learn from us, we also learn from our students—often! Do your best to see every new student as if she were a newborn baby. Try to see the wonderment of the musical world the way this baby does. It will give you a whole new perspective.

(2)

MISTERIOSO

Finding a Good Music Instructor

When I don't practice for one day, I know it; when I don't practice for two days, my friends know it; and when I don't practice for three days, the whole world knows it.

—Anton Rubenstein, pianist

PRELUDE

"Mr. Johnston is so old fashioned. I ask questions, but he never answers them. He talks to me like I'm stupid or something. I hate him. I hate going to those lessons. He's always criticizing me. I really can't stand him."

"Maybe he's just trying to teach you how to play the clarinet the right way, Timmy."

"No, Dad, he's really weird. I ask questions, and he tells me not to ask so many questions. At the last lesson all I asked him was whether he could tell how hard I practiced a piece, because I really spent hours at it. Every single day I worked on it as hard as I could. He got so angry because I interrupted the lesson to ask him something. D'ya know what he said to me?"

"No, what did he say?" asked Timmy's dad.

"He said that I should be quiet, and he'd tell me when it sounded like I practiced it. He made me feel so bad, because I really worked at it all week. And I think it was a lot better at the lesson. He never gives me credit for anything I do. Never! He never says anything is better. And this was better. I know it."

"That doesn't sound good, Timmy. Are you sure about this?"

"Of course I'm sure. You know, Dad, he's told me that I'm lazy, and sometimes he even calls me names. Last week he called me stupid a couple of times. I think he hates me. . . . And did you know he doesn't want to teach me jazz?"

"But that's why you wanted to study clarinet—to learn jazz."

"Right, Dad. Exactly. Would you call him and talk to him, please?"

"Okay, but if you're wrong . . ."

"Trust me, Dad. I'm not wrong about this. You'll see."

"Hello, Mr. Johnston. What's this I hear about your not wanting to teach Tim jazz? And he tells me that you have been kind of rough on him and don't answer his questions and— "

(Screaming) "Now, you listen here, Mr. Simon. I know how to handle Tim. Tim is *always* asking questions, hundreds and hundreds of questions, and I don't have time for all that nonsense. I'm much too busy. Tim spends half the teaching hour asking questions. And he never practices, no matter how much I talk to him about it, and he never listens to anything I tell him, and he's always talking, and he's lazy, and he's really lucky I don't toss him out on his ear. And did you know he wants to study jazz?" (Talking faster and faster) "He won't practice what I give him to learn, and he wants to learn jazz. You just can't begin to understand how hard I try with him, but there's no getting through to that boy. I'm at my wit's end. He's just plain— "

(Interrupting) "Thank you, Mr. Johnston. I think I understand now. Tim won't be coming for lessons any more."

FOR EVERYONE

The first step in beginning music lessons is finding a really good instructor. As a matter of fact, the first step in beginning any kind of lessons is finding a good instructor. Good teachers make lessons fun, exciting, and exhilarating. Students look forward to the lessons. The quickest way to turn someone off is to get an inadequate teacher.

Regardless of whether the student is beginning, intermediate, or advanced, child or adult, get the best instructor you can.

A Few Case Histories

Over the years we have heard hundreds of horror stories about the lessons students had in the past. One older lady said, "When I was a child, my teacher hit my hands with a ruler every time I hit a wrong note."

Another noted, "My teacher never told me *why* I had to do certain things on the instrument; he just said 'Go home and practice it.' I always wanted to know the reasons for his instructions, but he never took the time to explain them."

Still another said, "My mother hired an eighteen-year-old boy to teach me guitar because the lessons were cheap. I was just starting out, and my mom thought I didn't need 'good' lessons. She said that she would get me 'good' lessons later if I continued to show interest."

Although the neighborhood kid evidently played guitar reasonably well, he didn't have the foggiest idea about how to teach. He'd come to the

child's house, ostensibly to give a lesson, and spend the teaching hour playing a video game while the child played the guitar. Eventually, the parent walked in and saw the "teacher" playing a video game instead of teaching. That was the end of the lessons. When the student decided to try music instruction again, he was adamant about not wanting guitar. His first experience left a bad taste in his mouth. Actually, it was fortunate that he still wanted to study music at all.

Esther was twenty-three years old when she decided to return to music instruction. She had studied voice as an eleven-year-old child and had developed polyps on her vocal cords. It seems that the teacher had tried to force the immature voice to imitate the sound of various rock stars in hopes of getting the child into a major competition. As a result, Esther's voice was damaged for many years. It was only as an adult that the doctors allowed her to sing again.

FOR PARENTS

As in any endeavor, the right teacher can motivate and help develop a student's highest potential. The wrong one can turn a person off forever. Of course, the student must do a great deal *after* finding a good teacher, but the first step is *finding* the teacher. Following are some ideas and suggestions to help you on your way.

What to Look For

- Call the local colleges and universities. Speak to the dean of music at length about your needs. Get recommendations for well-qualified teachers known in the area. Musician-educators almost always know other musician-educators in the community, at least by reputation. In addition, most musicians are contract workers. Those who play in orchestras also often teach at the local colleges and privately. Call the local musicians' union and speak to the president or director, who also should be able to give you some leads. Don't hire some local garage-band musician to teach you or someone in your family. Finding a really good instructor at the start of one's musical education is certainly as important as (and perhaps even more important than) having a good instructor later on in advanced musical study. Good instruction insures a solid musical foundation and helps to cultivate interest, desire, and the drive to succeed.

- Look for a patient but strict instructor. The more exacting a teacher, the quicker a student learns. Good instructors encourage questions from students. They explain things in many different ways until they are certain that the student understands, and they couch their explanations in ways that enthuse the student.
- Note the instructor's personality. An instructor should be tough but fair, demanding but not demeaning. The teacher should demonstrate a great love for music and teaching and a sincere regard for the student without ever becoming overly familiar. In addition, think about whether the personality of the instructor will be compatible with the personality of the student. Good chemistry between the instructor and the student is crucial. If the student does not relate well to the instructor, no matter how wonderfully the instructor teaches, the student will not learn as well.
- Find out about the teacher's educational, teaching, and performing background. Don't be afraid to ask questions. Ask to see diplomas, certificates, awards, and other documentation. Has the teacher had specific training in teaching? How recent is that training, and how long has the teacher been teaching?
- Ask lots of questions. Don't be intimidated by the instructor. Most good instructors are happy to tell you their teaching ideas, methods, and policies. Don't settle for answers like "We do whatever we have to do." It's your consumer dollar, and you are entitled to know what you are getting for it.
- How does the teacher teach? Can you watch a lesson? If you are allowed to watch a lesson, don't say anything. Just observe. Notice how the teacher acts with the student: whether he writes anything down for the student, how complete the explanations are, how well the student understands, how enthusiastic the student is, and the rapport between the teacher and the student.
- How many students does the instructor have? Is it possible to talk to some of them? Are group or private lessons offered? Are lessons offered on the days or evenings and times that suit your schedule?
- The teacher you select should have expertise in teaching the style of music you want at the level you need. While the basics of learning musical technique in any instrument is basically the same, ultimately students should be able to study the particular style of music they are interested in playing or singing. After they have learned basic technique, someone interested in singing rock or gospel should transfer to a rock or gospel teacher. Put another way, if you want to learn to play

ice hockey, you shouldn't have to learn figure skating; once you know the basics of ice skating, you should go to someone who specializes in teaching ice hockey.

- Find out about the teacher's organization affiliations. Most instructors are affiliated with professional organizations and are actively involved in their meetings, activities, and conferences. Most of these organizations offer evaluations, competitions, juries, and other incentive programs to help motivate students.
- Does the teacher perform professionally somewhere? If you can, attend a performance. (Take earplugs if it's a rock performance.) But keep in mind that a good performer may not necessarily make a good teacher, while a good teacher may not necessarily be a good performer. Ideally, look for both strengths in one person.
- Ask for and check the instructor's references. Look the instructor up on the Internet, and check for any relevant information. Call local music stores, schools, and others in the music community to ask about the instructor's methods and reputation.

Four Important Things to Look Out For

- Find out if the prospective teacher has a troubling background: a rap sheet with the police department, complaints by former clients, or any kind of buzz about drugs, alcohol, or abuse. If the answer is yes to any of these, run, do not walk, away from that instructor.
- Does the instructor claim to teach all instruments and styles? Most teachers are specialists. They teach one or two types of music. Generally, teachers who teach jazz don't teach classical. Voice teachers who teach classical usually don't teach rock. Those who claim to teach all instruments and all styles may not play or teach any of them very well. Ordinarily, a good teacher will play a few instruments, often all in the same instrument family, but not always. For instance, a woodwind player may play all the woodwinds, but it is a little more unusual for a clarinetist to also play a tuba. Brass players and teachers generally stick to brass, and woodwind players and teachers generally stay with woodwinds. Pianists often play organ, harpsichord, and keyboards. A violinist may also play viola, and a cellist may also play acoustic bass. (Incidentally, watch out for ukulele players. There was one who started out as an acoustic bass player. When the bass got dirty, he put it in the washing machine and it shrank. Now it's a ukulele. My apologies to all ukulele players, I just couldn't resist a little play on the teeny ukulele.)

- Ask if you will be allowed to observe your child's lessons. If you are not, that should send up a warning flag for you. Whether a parent is in the room or not should be the parent's choice, not the teacher's. (Of course, if you, yourself, are the student and you're not allowed in the teaching room, then that in itself should speak volumes.) Seriously, if the teaching room is really small and would not comfortably accommodate a third person in it, that would be a legitimate reason for the teacher to ask you, the parent, to remain outside. Then again, that might send up another warning.

- Good instructors are continually upgrading their teaching skills. Some instructors who do not belong to any organizations are still in the dark ages, and don't believe they need to upgrade their skills. While it is not necessary to bring into play all the technology available today, it is always best if an instructor knows what is on the cutting edge and understands how to use it, should the need arise. Notice if the instructor is either so old-fashioned or so off-the-wall-experimental that you become uncomfortable. Chances are that if the instructor turns you off, your child will feel awkward with that instructor, too.

Other Important Questions

The following questions refer specifically to the kind and quality of lessons the instructor offers. Although you may not recognize the importance of the answers, and, in fact, may not even care, ask the questions anyway. They are very important and will increase in importance as the lessons evolve.

- Does the teacher know and teach theory in addition to playing the particular instrument? Besides learning how to play a musical instrument, students need to know "what, where, when, why, and how." Teachers who don't teach theory as part of the lesson are not offering the whole deal. Theory is the mechanics—the grammar—of why we do what we do in music. "What is the difference between a key signature and a scale?" "When doesn't a whole note get four beats?" "What's the difference between a chord and a triad?" "Where is middle C on the violin?" and "Why does the viola play in the alto clef?" are all questions answered by music theory.

- Does the instructor teach students to read music or only to improvise? Improvisation is a method of playing or singing or creating music by ear without learning to read the notes. Improvisation is a wonderful skill and ought to be learned. But because it is only part of what students need to know, it should be taught only after the student is fluent in reading music. Just as a student should learn to *play* music before composing music, the student should learn to *read* music before learning to improvise. If an instructor only teaches to improvise without teaching first to read music, find another instructor.

- Does the instructor only teach by rote? Even in the beginning students must learn to read music and not play or sing just by imitation. There is a story about an American scientist who went to Russia to give a lecture. Instead of having a simultaneous translator, he opted to learn to recite his lecture in Russian phonetically without knowing anything about the language. With some practice, he learned his speech flawlessly, the lecture went beautifully, and everyone understood what he had to say . . . that is, until the time came for questions from the audience. In the moment that the first person asked a question in Russian, the scientist realized the error he had made: he could recite the speech, but he didn't understand one word of the question.

- Does the instructor have regular incentive and follow-up programs like tests, progress reports, juries, and student recitals? Frustration and irritation build up easily in students. Working toward concerts and other occasions to demonstrate progress helps to develop pride, a sense of self-worth, and confidence. Students generally look forward to these little mini-milestones. They serve to encourage and inspire even greater achievement.

- Does the teacher encourage ensemble playing? Students often feel very lonely and isolated when they practice and appreciate the opportunity to play with others. Teachers who encourage ensemble playing in addition to regular private lessons, even at a very elementary level, add several positive elements to the musical experience. Ensemble playing:

  ○ makes the students feel that they are part of a peer group,
  ○ adds a social element to the musical endeavor and makes it more fun,
  ○ gives students an understanding of the need for teamwork and protecting and helping each other,
  ○ enhances an understanding of rhythm, and
  ○ teaches the student to listen to what the others are doing in relation to his own playing.

Most instrumentalists can play as part of a duet, trio, or quartet or with an elementary student band or orchestra after a relatively short while. Find out if that instructor encourages playing in ensembles. If so, that's a real plus. The student will stick with music lessons a lot longer, if he can play with someone else, especially a peer.

- Does the teacher teach in the location that you wish to learn? Will he or she come to wherever you live? Is the teaching site farther away than you want to travel? In some cases, it is more convenient for a teacher to come to your home. However, to obtain the services of a really good instructor, it is often worth the trouble to go to wherever that teacher is. Another point to be considered is that a student often concentrates better when he is not on his own turf. At the instructor's place there are no telephones ringing, no infants crying, and no extraneous distractions.
- Does the teacher evaluate students before acceptance to determine aptitude, interest, musical strengths and weaknesses, and placement? Such a test often helps a student choose the instrument he really wants. Have you ever heard the statement, "My mother made me study the piano when I was a kid, and I hated it"? No student should have to study an instrument he doesn't like. A preliminary aptitude test often helps in the selection of the best instrument. It also gives the instructor a window into the student's natural strengths and weaknesses and indicates the student's personality. It helps to know, in advance, if a student is overactive, learning-challenged, or has any specific problems that need attention. All in all, it makes for better teaching and better learning. If a prospective instructor thinks such a test is unnecessary and a waste of time, you should look elsewhere.
- Is the teacher capable of teaching the very young or the very old or have a preference for teaching one or the other? Teachers who are particularly good with children aren't necessarily adept at teaching older students, and vice versa. If your needs are for a teacher who teaches the versa, a teacher who specializes in something else isn't going to be helpful.
- Can the teacher work with exceptional children or adults? The specially gifted and the emotionally, physically, or mentally-challenged all have special needs and require a very special kind of teaching. Does the instructor know how to recognize and handle learning problems, hyperactive students, or whatever your specific needs require?
- History of music and small anecdotes also spur interest. Does the teacher teach smatterings of music history and pepper explanations with little stories about the compositions, composers, or performers?

- Does the instructor tell the parent how to help reinforce the teaching without making the parent also learn to play the instrument? Does he also tell the parent what *not* to do, so as not to turn the student off? There are many things a parent can do to encourage a student, and there are a slew of things the parent should *never* do. Numerous studies indicate that family attitude, support, and involvement are important factors in a student's ability to successfully learn to play an instrument.
- Does the instructor have reference books and some kind of music library if needed?
- Is the instructor familiar with the music available for the student's level?
- Does the instructor write down assignments so that the student knows what to do? Do the assignments include positive comments as well as constructive criticism? Comments by the teacher should always include what's good about the student's work as well as what needs to be improved and should have specific instructions about how to fix whatever needs to be fixed. One student told us, "My teacher never told me when I was doing something wrong. So I never learned what was good and what was bad. He just told me, 'Great lesson; see you next week.'" Another said, "My teacher always criticized me. She never once complimented me on anything I did. It made me feel as if I couldn't do anything right." While it is true that students must be corrected when they are doing something wrong, it is equally important for them to know when they are doing something right.

Two Final Thoughts

- Don't be swayed by cheap prices. If it takes a student twelve hours of lessons to learn what a more talented teacher can teach in three, lessons that seemed cheaper at first glance may actually cost you more money in the long run.
- Don't be taken in by promises to make your child a star or promises to teach him to play any instrument or sing in merely a few weeks. There are no shortcuts. Learning music needs time, patience, and lots of dedication. Frankly, it takes years, many more years than most people are prepared to put into it. But the good news is that the musical life of a musician is practically forever. Professional musicians continue to play well up into their eighties. Wanda Landowska, the renowned harpsichordist, gave her farewell performance at the age of eighty-

eight. Arthur Rubinstein played his last concert at ninety-four. On the other hand, athletes have a performing life of eight, ten, maybe twelve years. After that? . . . At that rate, ten or eleven years training to be a musician seems comparatively short. And, yes, we call it "training," whether it's for a hobby, therapy, or a career. Would you really want inferior music education just because you don't plan to be a professional? A good instructor teaches well, no matter what the purpose is.

FOR STUDENTS

If you are an older student and it is your responsibility to find an instructor for *yourself*, the information in the *For Parents* section above is as important for you as it is for parents. A little before-hand research goes a long way toward getting the best value for your time, effort, and money.

FOR INSTRUCTORS

When prospective students or their parents ask for information, be direct in your answers and offer responses even to those questions they don't know to ask. Give a brief overview of your teaching style and methods. Show any diplomas you may have, and discuss your credentials and experience. Let them know about organizations with which you are affiliated (and in which you present your students). Tell them about programs you offer, including tests, competitions, juries, evaluations, and student recitals. Be professional but not authoritarian. Be warm, approachable, and cordial but not overly familiar. From the very first contact, demonstrate that you have the training, experience, and teaching skills necessary to pass on your knowledge to others with patience, understanding, and respect. One last thought—look at the suggestions above. If there are any areas in your studio or in your teaching methods that could use improvement, consider making those improvements soon.

3

ALLEGRO ASSAI

Four Wheels and an Engine—Getting the Equipment

I get very nervous when I am making records. When test records are made, I know that I can hear them played back to me and everything is all right. But when the stage is set for the final recording, I realize that this is for good. I get nervous, and my hands get tense.

—Serge Rachmaninoff, pianist

PRELUDE

"Hello, Mrs. Brown. I hope I'm not disturbing you, but I wanted to tell you that Susan had a really tough time at her lesson this week. She didn't do well at all. Every time she tried to play on the E-string of the violin, she couldn't do it. Every note on that string was wrong. Did she practice during the week? Is something going on at home that I should know about?"

"No, everything is fine here. Busy like always. But I heard Susan practicing."

"Well, I don't know what caused it, but she had trouble on all the notes on that string in every piece she played. You know, she never brings her violin to class so she always has to use the school violin that's here. Is there something wrong with her violin?"

"Hmmm. I don't know. I remember about a month ago that she told me something needed to be fixed on it, but she hasn't said anything since. I figured it was okay. Just a minute, it's right here; let me look at it. . . . Umm, it looks okay to me. 'Course I don't know. . . . Umm, how many strings is it supposed to have?"

"Four. Why?"

"Well, it has only three. Do you suppose that's what she meant when she said something was wrong with it?"

(In a disturbed tone of voice) "Violins are supposed to have four strings, Mrs. Brown. . . . Susan's only has three strings. When can you get it fixed?"

"Well, as soon as I can. I'm sorry, but I'm really very busy between work and the family. I'll try sometime within the next few weeks, anyway.

Besides, Susan said she's not sure she wants to continue her music lessons anyway."

"Hmm. Do you suppose that could be because her violin doesn't work properly? She can't practice on the E-string if there isn't one, Mrs. Brown. That's why she has been having so much trouble. I think you'll find that if she has a working instrument she won't want to stop lessons."

"Okay. I'll take the instrument to the violin shop today. I'll get it fixed for her by the next lesson, and I'm sorry for taking so long. Frankly, I had no idea how important it was."

FOR EVERYONE

Okay, so now you've found what we hope will be a great music instructor. The next step is obtaining an instrument. Beginning and even intermediate students don't need to buy the Cadillac or Rolls Royce of instruments. All they need is "four wheels and an engine." Of course, the instrument must be in good working order. If it isn't, it must be fixed before the student can practice on it. Students shouldn't be expected to practice on an instrument that doesn't function correctly. Warped wood, bows with hanging hairs, sticking valves, missing parts, sticking keys, broken hammers? They all need to be fixed as soon as the damage occurs. Nothing frustrates a student faster than trying to practice on an instrument that needs repair. Nothing!

There are plenty of instrument repair shops. Look in the phone book or on the Internet, or ask the teacher for the name of someone. Chances are good that if the instructor teaches and plays the instrument, the teacher will also know how and where to get it fixed, as well as the approximate cost of the repair.

FOR PARENTS

Don't go out to buy an instrument until *after* you've found, met, and spoken at length with the instructor. Instruments come in families. There's the string family, the woodwind family, the brass family, and the percussion family. Instruments in the string family must be sized for the student. No, I'm sorry, your five year old can't learn the upright acoustic bass, and the tuba is too big for him, also. A child is much too small to play such a large instrument.

Sizing Instruments

If your child is going to study a stringed instrument, ask the teacher what size to get for the child. Don't spend a fortune on it, and make sure the teacher *sees* the student before recommending what size to get. You can't just call up the teacher and say, "I have a six year old. What size violin does she need?" A tall four year old may need a larger instrument than a small six year old. Stringed instruments come in several sizes: full, three-quarter, half, quarter, eighth, and sixteenth. And, no, you can't use a full-size violin, put a stick on the end of it, and use it as a very small cello. In addition to sizes, instrument families also come in soprano, alto, tenor, and bass voices, like a chorus. Each instrument within any instrument family has a different range of sound—the smaller the instrument, the higher the pitch. In the string family, the violin is the soprano, viola is alto, the cello is tenor, and the bass is—you guessed it—the bass.

Purchasing a Stringed Instrument

You can purchase a reasonably good student violin for about $450 or so, and that generally includes the bow, case, and rosin. Teachers usually don't recommend the cheaper violins and violas, which generally can't be tuned very well, because when the student tries, the pegs don't hold or the strings break.

Most music stores have a program where you can buy a smaller-sized instrument and upgrade to larger sizes as the child grows. Of course, you can opt to purchase a well-cared-for second-hand instrument.

Student instruments can also be rented by the month. A good place to check out used musical instruments is a pawn shop, but be careful. Instruments sitting in second-hand shops for a while usually need some kind of repair. If you elect to buy one from that kind of store, try to bring the instructor or someone knowledgeable (about the instrument) with you who can tell you what kind of repair, if any, is needed. Sometimes the repair costs more than the instrument. Regardless of the place of purchase, whether it's new or used, the larger the instrument, the greater the cost. Incidentally, be prepared for strange sounds if your child is starting string lessons—think "cat in pain." A cello student similarly produces tones on the instrument that sound pained, but from a much larger cat.

An acoustic guitar comes in full, three-quarter, half, and eighth sizes. Most guitar instructors suggest that beginning students get a nylon-string acoustic guitar because it's easier to play and the strings don't hurt the fingers so much. Steel strings often make tender fingers bleed, and bleeding all over the fingerboard isn't very conducive to making a student want to practice.

As with any instrument, don't go out and spend a thousand dollars for an electric guitar, amp, case, tuner, and mic. It's just not necessary. In the beginning, think simple. Just make sure the instrument is sized correctly and that everything works well. Incidentally, when the time *does* come to get an electric guitar, you'll need an amplifier with it because you just can't hear the sound without one. Of course, if the student doesn't play very well, not having an amplifier just might be an advantage.

Many folks think that an electric bass is just a low-sounding guitar. It's not. An electric bass is more like an upright acoustic bass than a guitar. Like the acoustic bass, it has only four strings, whereas the guitar has six strings, and sometimes twelve. The one big difference between the acoustic bass and the electric bass is that the electric bass player doesn't use a bow. (She doesn't use any arrows either.) Rather, she plucks the strings.

Woodwind Instruments

A student should be between seven and nine years old when beginning a woodwind instrument because of the breath required to play it and because woodwind and brass instruments are generally not sizable. Flute teachers usually suggest that students wait to begin the transverse flute (the silver one that goes sideways) until their arms are long enough to reach both ends of it. Otherwise, they have to insert a U-shaped extension that brings certain valves of the instrument within reach of the student. That extension is about $800, and once the student's arms are long enough to reach both ends easily, it is removed, never to be used again. Usually the extension is more expensive than the flute itself and is not worth the price, considering the short period of time the student will actually use it (probably not more than a year).

Oh—and a piccolo is *not* a small flute. It's a whole different instrument, higher in sound and more difficult to play. Similarly, the little *recorder* (oh, you know, the instrument kids play in kindergarten that sounds a lot like a squawking hen) isn't the same as the flute that everyone is familiar with. It's actually a relative of the tin whistle and the ocarina and was popular in the medieval era.

A beginning woodwind student probably will find a clarinet easier to play than any of the other woodwind instruments, because it requires less breath control and less air (breathing capacity of the student, not the air in the atmosphere).

The most difficult instrument of the woodwind family to master is the oboe. Of course, when we speak of ease or difficulty of learning, consider that each instrument has its own difficulties and its own areas where it is easier, eventually evening out the comparative difficulty among all instruments.

The Brass Family

Most students probably should be over the age of eight or nine when beginning a brass instrument, because more air and lung capacity is needed

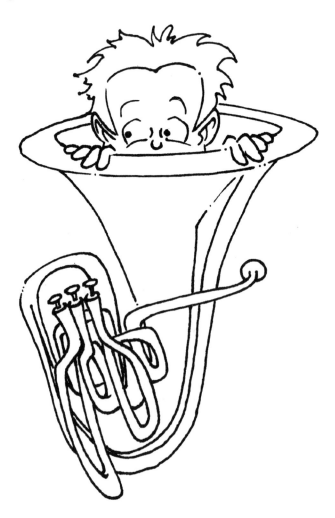

for a brass instrument than for a woodwind. Hmm . . . your child is six, but he's five feet eleven inches tall. Well, in that case, maybe! But don't try to get a tuba for your eight-year-old son. It's just too big, unless, maybe, he could use it for a cave in which to hide. (Then, when he is fifteen or so, if he hasn't already broken the instrument, he could learn to play it.) As for the trombone, since its extension is considerable, it's better to wait until the child's arms are longer. On the other hand, he might do well with a baritone horn or a French horn.

Percussion

Most children love to bang on a drum. They think that when they bang on a drum they are "playing music." Because of that, many of them ask for drum lessons. Learning to play drums doesn't teach the student how to read music, because most drums don't play notes; they play rhythm. Therefore, students don't learn everything they need in order to become musically proficient. To prevent that, teachers often suggest that a child should study a "tuned" instrument, like a violin, piano, flute, or guitar, before starting drums to allow time to become fluent in music notation, melodic ideas, and rhythmic concepts.

Another thing to consider: most students hear drums as part of a band or a larger group of instruments. Most drums don't sound quite the same when they are played alone because they don't play individual melody lines. As a result, students may soon become disillusioned and disinterested in continuing their lessons. Learning to play drums is wonderful and should be encouraged, but it is usually better to start instruction on an instrument that requires proficiency in music notation before taking on the drums. If a student is absolutely adamant about learning percussion first, it would be beneficial for her to learn the mallet instruments first—xylophone, marimba, vibraphone, or glockenspiel—because they are tuned (each note has a different sound) and are configured like the keys of a piano keyboard.

Incidentally, there is a difference between the terms *drummer* and *percussionist*. A drummer plays drums, albeit many kinds of drums—drum set, high hat, and every instrument you can shake, rattle, or roll. Percussionists play all that and all the mallet instruments as well.

Pianos and Keyboards

When buying pianos and keyboards, the size of the instrument is unimportant. Even the shape is unimportant. What *is* important is how many keys it has, how big the keys are, and how those keys make their sound. The instrument should have eighty-eight keys. Keyboards with fewer notes confuse the student about where the middle of the instrument is. The keys should be full-size. Those little baby keyboards with the itty-bitty keys are good to put on someone's birthday cake, but they teach nothing to a beginning student. Since small keys don't grow the way the child's fingers grow, the child's sense of touch about the distance and size of the keys becomes distorted.

Many stores allow you to rent a console piano for several months and sometimes deduct the cost of the rental if you buy it. A console piano is one of those short, upright jobs, not the big, long pianos.

Some Confusing Terms

The keys on a piano should be *weighted*, *velocity sensitive*, and *full-size*. *Weighted* means that they feel like an acoustic piano key, not like the key on a computer keyboard; there is resistance when you push the note down.

Velocity sensitive means that if you hit the keys with more force the sound is correspondingly louder, and if you hit them with less force, the sound is softer. *Full-size* means, well, full-size.

Acoustic, Electronic, and Digital

Some people are a bit confused between the terms *acoustic* and *electric* (or *electronic*). *Acoustic* means there's nothing to plug in; you play the instrument as it is, it's completely mechanical, and the inside of the instrument has strings, felts, and hammers.

Electric (or *electronic*) means you have to plug the instrument in, and, if the power goes out, it won't work. (Incidentally, neither will your refrigerator.) On the other hand, if you have enough batteries for some electronic pianos, they'll work—at least until the batteries wear out. (Unfortunately, they won't help your refrigerator.)

A digital piano is a very sensitive instrument that gets plugged in, has many different kinds of controls, and often simulates the sound and touch of an acoustic piano so well that, to the novice, it's hard to tell the difference. It is usually complete in itself with built-in speakers and legs. And don't look for strings, hammers, and felts, because there aren't any. The inside of a digital piano looks more like the inside of a computer than a piano.

Pros of a Digital Piano

If you are thinking of buying an inexpensive piano instead of renting and are wondering which kind to get, acoustic or digital, you might be better off with a digital instrument if it's for a beginning or early-intermediate student. Here are some reasons:

- First of all, acoustic pianos need to be tuned about three times a year (at $75–$85 a pop), and strings and hammers break from time to time. Digitals don't ever need tuning. Strings and hammers can't break, because there aren't any.
- Acoustic pianos have a "piano" sound. That's it—one sound. Digitals have the option of many different sounds. Therefore, when the student tires of practicing on a "piano," she can change the sound to an organ, a harpsichord, strings, brass, or a combination of any of them.
- A digital console piano generally lasts longer than its acoustic counterpart and needs less maintenance. Conversely, when a digital piano does need to be repaired, the repair often costs more than fixing an acoustic piano.
- A digital console piano is generally a teeny bit smaller than a regular console and therefore needs less room, a real plus when you're pressed for space. Some of them are actually portable. Others are semi-portable.
- Some digitals can be plugged into a computer, and you can reinforce learning, listening, and other aspects of music instruction through interfacing computer programs.
- A digital console generally comes with earphones so that the student can practice without disturbing anyone else in the house. (In a condo or apartment, earphones keep the neighbors and the police from your door during late-night practice sessions.)

The Down Side of Digitals

The down side of digital pianos is that digital consoles don't have exactly the same touch or feel that an acoustic piano has (at least not as of this writing). Eventually, the student notices the difference and begins to prefer the acoustic touch and feel. However, that doesn't happen until somewhere around the middle-intermediate level or so. By that time the student should have a regular acoustic instrument. However, you might want to keep the digital instrument as well to provide some variety in sound, possibilities for experimentation, and portability.

Another Option

Another option is to purchase an eighty-eight-key digital keyboard with an adjustable stand. However, be careful: You can't just stick the keyboard on top of a table. The height of the table may be different from the height of a piano, which will cause the student to experience confusion and discomfort when subsequently playing on a regular instrument. Therefore, if you elect to purchase a full-size keyboard instead of a console or digital piano, set up the stand so that when the keyboard is on it, the height of the top of the white keys measures between 28.5 and 29.5 inches from the floor, the same height as a regular piano.

If there is more than one piano student in the house who sits at the piano, you might think about getting an adjustable bench that is adaptable to any size student.

Think Simple

Don't spend more than $1,500 for the instrument. If you can catch a sale, you can probably get one for less than $1,000. Forget the bells and whistles for now. In the beginning you don't need them anyway. A digital instrument (piano or keyboard) should have

- no more than four or five different instrument voices,
- a few rhythms that the student can play with,
- at least two pedals,
- built-in speakers,
- earphones,
- a metronome, if possible (a good idea, but not crucial; metronomes can be bought separately), and

- the ability to record and listen to what you play (also a good idea, but not crucial).

Incidentally, have you ever wondered why you can't buy diapers for a baby grand piano? Or why a baby grand never grows up to be an adult grand, no matter how long you have them? Or why a grand piano never gets old enough to become a great-grand piano?

About Organs

Someone who wants to study organ should probably start out with the piano, because the piano is less complicated. The organ has a lot more bells and whistles, and therefore students must coordinate many more elements in order to be able to play it successfully. For instance,

- organs usually have several manuals (keyboards, not how-to books), not just one,
- most organs have at least twelve pedals, so the student must learn how to coordinate the movement of the hands over several keyboards with the movement of the feet on pedals that she cannot see,
- the touch on an organ is also very different from that of a piano (as the keys on an organ depress like the keys on a computer keyboard), increasing the likelihood that the student will hit many more wrong notes than would happen on a piano (think of how many accidental typos happen on a computer), and
- if the student doesn't hold down a note during the movement from manual to manual, the sound of that note stops.

Therefore, generally speaking, starting out with the piano, which is a simpler instrument, will make it easier for the student to learn.

About Harps

Studying harp is also often more successful if the student starts out with the piano. Harp and piano share several similarities and one huge difference. Like pianists, harpists play the instrument with both hands on two sides of the instrument at the same time. Harp music also looks very much like piano music, because harpists read two lines of music at one time, the way pianists do. Most other instrumentalists read only one line of music at a time. However, there is a big difference in the placement of music for the harp. While pianists have the music directly in front of them, harpists must keep the music to the side of the instrument, making it more difficult to read. That's why it is better to start on the piano, so that any student beginning to play the harp will already be able to read notes fluently. Harps also come in different sizes and different kinds. There are folk harps, pedal harps, lever harps, concert harps, and lyres (the kind of harp the angels play), to name just a few. Oh, and please keep in mind that while most angels play harps, most harpists aren't angels. Quite a few of them are real devils, in fact.

FOR STUDENTS

If it is your responsibility to find your own instrument, then every word in the section marked *For Parents* is equally important for you. The only thing that changes is the remarks about sizing. Chances are that you won't need to think about sizing instruments, as you'll need one that is full-size.

FOR INSTRUCTORS

Parents and students look to their instructors to help them find a proper instrument. Try to give them the best and most complete information you can. If it is necessary to measure the student for an instrument, do so carefully. Write down the numbers for them and any information that the parent will need to buy the instrument, including the measurements. In some cases, parents may ask you to make a choice among a few instruments they have looked at or to help them find one at a pawn shop. If it is possible for you to go with them, then do so. It will help make them much more comfortable ("Even if *I* know zip about all this, I have someone with me who *does*").

If you cannot go with them to purchase the instrument, then try to provide them with as much information as you can. Offer to talk with them by phone while they are in the store; offer to talk with the salesperson, if necessary; do whatever you can to make them feel at ease. Remember that they feel as if they are in a strange world, dealing with strange people (and aren't all musicians strange people?), and they are very much off-balance.

Instructors, at one time or another, are so much more than teachers. We have to be psychologists, inspirational leaders, guides, mathematicians, story weavers, den mothers and fathers, doctors' helpers, substitute parents, exercise partners, confidantes, and sometimes (hopefully not too often) shoulders on which our students can cry. How appropriate, then, that when parents and students start out on this long musical journey, instructors give a leg up for that first big step—getting the instrument.

4

ALLEGRETTO

Starting Out on the Right Foot (or Hand)

Half the battle is learning to smile,
To hold up your head and lift up your chin;
Half the battle is picking up the pieces
And starting over again.

—Sidney Michael, "Ben Franklin in Paris"

PRELUDE

Delores was preparing for an audition for entrance into a magnet school specializing in the arts when her mother called to cancel her voice lessons.

"But why?" asked the instructor. "It's so close to the test. Why stop lessons a month before the audition? There's still a lot of work to do on the songs Delores will sing. Don't you want her to be the best she can?"

"She says that it's just too much pressure for her," said Delores's mother. "She has a lot to do. She has school and homework, and she complains that she doesn't have time to do all that practicing. She tells me that having lessons once a week is one thing. Having to practice every day is something else. She doesn't want to have to do practice."

"What does she think will happen if she gets into the magnet school?" the instructor asked. "There she'll have even more music practice. There'll be rehearsals, lessons, practicing at home, and performances. Doesn't she want to get into the school?"

Delores's mother answered sadly, "I don't know. She says she does, but she doesn't want to do the work at home. She said that it's really annoying for her to practice, because the family is in the same room at that time watching TV. Unfortunately, there's no other place for the family to go. That's where the TV is. She practices at night, when the family is home, so that's when they watch TV. Anyhow, she says she can get in without all that practicing. She figures she'll just sing for them, and that will be it. She thinks her voice is good enough that she doesn't have to practice. What can I do? She told me she doesn't want any more lessons. She said she just wants to 'go for it' and see what happens at the test . . ."

The instructor answered, "The trouble with that is that there are many other students trying to get into that school and there are only a few openings. Out of several hundred applying, the school will only take ten or twelve. Those they accept will be the ones who cared enough to be the best, those who prepared, the ones who did the practice."

"You're right, and I've tried and tried and tried to talk to her, but I can't do anything with her. She absolutely won't listen to me. She doesn't even want to talk about it. She says she's done. She just wants to wing it and whatever happens, happens."

FOR EVERYONE

There are some general rules that will help every person beginning music lessons. Whether you are the parent of a young child, an adult student, or an older person going back to music lessons (or just starting out), it is very important to create a quiet environment in which to practice. (If you are pregnant and want your unborn child to learn how to practice even before it's born, you're reading the wrong book.)

FOR PARENTS

As I said in the previous chapter, make sure the instrument the student uses is in good working order. Instruments that have sticking valves, tuning pegs that don't hold, broken reeds, or keyboards that require adjusting or fixing are a source of real frustration.

Providing a good working instrument for a child is crucial, especially if the child knows something is wrong with it and yet *you* keep putting off getting it fixed. That's the fast track to blaming *you* for not practicing. Having one note that doesn't play soon escalates into ten fingers that *refuse* to play because they know the instrument is "broken" and mommy or daddy is too mean to get it fixed. This leads to screaming matches you cannot win and a nasty, stubborn scene that could easily have been avoided by one phone call to the technician.

Think about this: if every time you hit a particular note you know *before* you hit it that the note is going to stick, gradually the body will learn to flinch or avoid playing the note just before the moment that the note should be struck. Mentally, the hand learns to stay away from the note that is going to sound nasty or not sound at all. That's not the message you want to give the fingers. One of the first things the fingers have to learn is to play the notes evenly and without hesitation.

A Case History

Marissa's pedal on her piano at home didn't work. As a result of having to practice without pedal, she couldn't develop the hand-foot coordination necessary for pedal technique. Even when she came for lessons and had access to a piano with a working pedal she couldn't make use of it because she didn't know how to use the hands and feet together. Teaching her how didn't help, because she had no way to practice the technique at home. Eventually, the parents got the instrument fixed, but by that time it had set Marissa's progress back quite a bit, and she was very frustrated.

Creating an Environment

Create a quiet, pleasant place to practice with plenty of air, light, and preferably a window—not for escape (unless that becomes really necessary), but so that the student doesn't feel isolated or imprisoned. If the weather is cold, make sure there is enough heat in the room to be comfortable over a long period of time. If it's hot, make sure the air conditioner is on and working. (See above paragraph about broken equipment.) The paragraph that ends with "I hate practice" often starts with "It's freezing in here" or "It's so hot here."

The practice room should be out of the way of general traffic. Any student will become distracted if big brother runs through the room yelling, "Did you see my car keys, Mom?" or, "Can I borrow your jacket, Dad?" or if little sister gets into a fight with little brother. Speaking of general traffic, practicing an instrument in the middle of the street with oncoming cars is probably a bad idea. If the student plays well, the drivers may stop to listen, but if the student plays badly, the drivers may run him over.

Turning on the TV in the room where a student is practicing (even if the sound is very quiet) is also a really bad idea. Even just watching a silent video will distract. No amount of "Just concentrate, Joey; don't pay attention to us" is going to make the teeniest dent in the amount of distraction, annoyance, and frustration that this scenario causes. Ideally, besides the student, the only other person who belongs in the room should be the parent who supervises the practice (if the student is young enough to require one). The parent should be supportive, encouraging, and able to help with reading and interpreting the assignments. It helps a lot if the parent has an understanding of how difficult it is to sit at the instrument for a long stretch. Be prepared to come up with ways to keep the student patient and focused. When a child wants to leave practice, a simple, "Wow, that sounded wonderful; can you do it five times more just as well as you did now? Come on, let's try—I bet you can," does wonders toward encouraging another fifteen or thirty minutes of practice.

Practice Is Lonely

Practice is often a lonely business. Although it is not always possible for a parent to consistently stay in the room during a child's practice sessions, try to be nearby at least as often as possible. Offer compliments and encouragement freely, regularly, and enthusiastically. Even if you absolutely can't be around while the student is practicing, make time to sit down and listen to the student's practice several times a week. Even if you know nothing about music, you can offer encouragement like, "It's great how you can make music out of all those dots."

The parent is not expected to learn the instrument along with the young child (although there are some methods that do advocate this). However, there are things the parent can learn to do that will be helpful to the student. For instance, the more the parent varies the practice whenever (or even before) the student seems fatigued or bored, the more successful the student's practice will be. If the child is working with percussion instruments like drums, shakers, or tambourines and seems to be getting antsy, switch to finding notes on the instrument. Suggest writing notes, clapping rhythms, or reciting lines and spaces. Ask the child to make happy music, sad music, and mysterious music. When you change the activity often enough, you minimize frustration and rebellion. And remember to always encourage creativity.

While we are mentioning that "practice is often a lonely business," let's talk for a moment about group instruction versus private instruction. Group instruction is cheaper than private lessons and often much more social. However, since the teacher must use the slowest student as the common denominator, quicker students don't learn as readily as they might in private lessons. In addition, the instructor doesn't have much time for individual students. Regardless of whether the lessons are group or one-on-one, when it comes time for the student to practice his assignment at home, he *still* is alone when he practices.

Children under the age of eight need someone to sit with them during practice. The family member who is part of the support system should try to do whatever helps the student. The adult can help explain what should be done and how to do it and keep the child focused and interested. And when that moment comes (and it will) that your child calls out to you, "Come see what I can do!" "Listen to how this sounds," or "Watch me," stop whatever you are doing and run, do not walk, *run* to her side to watch, listen, and applaud as if she had just won a gold medal. Your support and enthusiasm is vital to the child's progress.

Older children also need someone within earshot to call out comments that indicate that there is another being besides the student who is listening and cares. Family interest and support go a long way toward motivating the student. With musical aptitude, productive practice, and your encouragement, playing music will become a natural part of your child's life.

How Long to Practice, How Often to Practice

Encourage the student to practice *every day*, including weekends. Don't suggest that if the student practices well all week you'll let her off the hook on weekends. Practice is not a synonym for punishment (although sometimes it seems like it is). The more consistently the student practices, the faster the advancement. If a student goes two or three days without practicing, the mind and the hands unlearn everything that was learned.

Remove all clocks and watches from the room. This may sound silly, but when clocks are in the room, eyes are drawn to it. Unconsciously, we think about how long we practice. That's not good. What we should be thinking about is what we can accomplish in the time we have. Even the supervising parent should not be thinking about time spent, if possible. Who cares if your daughter is late for swimming class or your son is late for soccer? You're sitting with your other child helping her to practice *music*! Of course, I'm just joking; but the more everyone can ignore the clocks around the house when someone is practicing, the more concentrated that practicing will be.

How long a student practices every day is relatively unimportant. Obviously, the longer one practices, the faster one progresses. However, a lesser amount of practice, conscientiously and consistently done every day, is actually more valuable than practicing longer one day and then skipping the next day or two. Encourage practice every day, and discourage attention to the *amount* of practice.

Schedule a consistent daily time for practice when the student isn't tired, whenever possible. Encourage the student to practice at the same time, but don't be rigid. Sometimes the best way to schedule practice is to divide it into several segments throughout the day (i.e., before school, after school, before going to bed). If the child shows signs of fatigue or boredom, it is better to stop practice and try again later in the day. There is nothing wrong

with practicing two, three, or even four times a day in small time segments if that works best for the child.

Students often say they just can't practice because other things are happening in their lives: "I have finals this week." "I have three tests tomorrow." "Ah, gee, I'm tired; I had three tests today." "I have a project due tomorrow that I have to finish." "All my friends are going out tonight, and I want to go with them." And so on. The truth is that no one ever *has* enough time to do practice. If a student wants to learn anything, then she is going to have to make time, not *wait* 'til she has *time*.

Ways to Be Helpful

When the instructor tells the student to get new music, make sure you get it as quickly as possible. Don't find excuses for why you couldn't get to the store. The student is waiting for it and is all hyped up about it. Maybe it's a favorite song, or a book that represents a promotion to the next level of learning. In any case, the student is excited, and if the new material doesn't arrive soon, she gets upset and loses interest. If the music isn't available at the local music stores, order it online. There are hundreds of music stores online, and individual books are not expensive. If you can't get it through one website, go to another. In today's world, where the furthest country is a couple of keystrokes away, there are just no excuses for procrastination. The point is that when the teacher says to get new music you must get it promptly.

Offer a snack or a meal before practice begins. That statement doesn't require a long-winded explanation, does it? You know what a snack is— cookies, milk, a sixteen-ounce steak, a 9 × 13–inch pan of lasagna—whatever makes the student happy. Teachers of wind instruments and voice teachers disagree with this idea. Therefore, never feed a voice student before he sings. (Maybe he'll be too nauseous to eat *after* he sings, too.) Make sure students don't eat or drink while practicing. Anything falling onto or into instruments can seriously and sometimes permanently damage them (the instruments, not the students). Also be careful that there is no residue of sugar or food in wind instruments; it causes the metal to corrode or can be ingested when the student breathes.

Encourage the child to go to the bathroom *before* beginning practice. Otherwise you'll be surprised at how many times the student will have to go *during* practice. It's right up there with the excuses the same child has for not going to sleep at night: "I'm thirsty." "I'm hungry." "I have to go to the bathroom." "There are monsters in my room." The only thing ostensibly missing from the practice room would be the monsters, and yet I'm sure that some child, somewhere, has already used that excuse.

Put all toys out of sight of a young child to minimize distractions. A child's comfort zone lies in the things the child finds familiar. If practicing makes a young child uneasy, he will retreat to his toys. And if the toys are readily available, that's where the child will prefer to be. It takes time for a child to accept and want new things, whether that new thing is a food, an activity, or a musical instrument. Don't make the music lessons compete with something comfortingly familiar.

For very young children (eighteen months to two years) enrolled in a program where percussion instruments or other music supplies are used, store all the instruments and supplies out of the sight of the child, except during relegated practice time. When the child expresses interest in using them, say, "Yes, this is a good time for music practice."

If the student is willing, informal concerts for family and friends are a wonderful reward for all the work that has been done. The oohing and ah-ing from the audience is terrific inspiration for the novice student musician, worth at least another few months of diligent practice.

Don't force the student to play for family and friends if the student *doesn't* enjoy it. Forcing an unwilling student to perform creates unnecessary stress and discomfort. The child may become overly anxious, resulting in a poor performance, which, in turn, can turn the student off to musical study altogether. Remember, the purpose of all of this is for your child to "tune in and turn on" to music. If it does the opposite, something is seriously wrong.

Expose the Child to Music

Expose your child to a wide range of music, including concerts and recitals of every kind, so that both of you become familiar with many styles of music. It will be an experience that is fun for everyone.

Help your child build a personal library of sheet music, CDs, and DVDs related to different kinds of music, composers, and musicians. Teach the child to take care of the collection so that it lasts for many years. Many musicians have music and recorded material from more than fifty years ago. Okay, so the music is old, but the musicians are even older.

Listen to the CDs and DVDs along with your child, and look through the music together.

When sheet music becomes raggedy, either restore it with acid-free scotch tape or, if it isn't a financial hardship (most beginning books are under $10), replace it. Students shouldn't have to piece together music in order to be able to read it.

Don't allow any debate or fight about how to practice. That's the fastest way to make music lessons a battleground. If there is a question about what the assignment is or what the instructor wants the student to do, call the teacher and clarify the assignment. Record the lessons and assignments to minimize confusion so that you can listen to the tape and hear exactly what the instructor said. However, even then it is very easy to misinterpret what you think the instructor wants the student to do. Therefore, if you still are confused after listening to the tape, call the instructor. A few minutes of discussion on the phone (or online via e-mail) with the teacher will resolve any issues and defuse what could become a struggle. Asking the teacher questions settles any dispute amicably, and it is certainly better than waiting until the next lesson to find out what you should have done. Therefore, don't hesitate to call or contact the instructor if you have questions. Keep asking until you are sure you understand the answers. If the instructor objects to such calls, find another instructor.

FOR STUDENTS

Again, everything in the section marked for parents is equally applicable to students who are adults or seniors.

A Working Instrument

An adult student will be put off by an instrument that doesn't work properly. In addition, the adult will continually be reminded that it needs to be fixed and will feel distracted and guilty. Besides, it's just easier to play the instrument if everything works properly. Therefore, if something is wrong with your instrument, fix the problem or replace the instrument as soon as possible.

Avoiding Boredom

Likewise, the comments about varying practice to avoid boredom, tedium, and fatigue are just as important for adults as for children. Find ways to vary practice whenever it threatens to become too monotonous. Change to another piece or work on rhythm, notation, speed, memory, or dynamics.

To Be or Not to Be . . . Alone

Adults, like children, may prefer to have someone in the room while they are practicing, either for moral support or company or to be a sounding board as they play the piece through. The applause given to children when they perform is just as rewarding for an adult (only *maybe* the adult won't admit it). Of course, you may be someone who prefers to be alone during practice. Become familiar with whatever makes you most comfortable, and, wherever possible, try to apply that when you practice.

Starting from Scratch

If you are an adult professional, well-respected in your own field, who has decided to study music, be prepared to feel a little unbalanced and out of your comfort zone. Adults who have established themselves in professional fields often find it difficult to take direction from an instructor who tells them what to do and how to do it. Such students are not used to *taking* orders; they're used to *giving* them. The professional adult often feels pressed for time because, in her own specialty, she is extremely busy. Such a student often has a preconceived idea of what she needs to learn and wants to learn just that. Such a student doesn't want to accept any idea that she might benefit from instruction in an area that she hasn't even thought about. In addition, a professional sometimes becomes upset when the instructor tells her to buy music or do theory homework. Such a person probably hasn't done written homework or bought books since college. The secretary, the valet, the assistant, and the butler do all that.

If you are a well-established professional, once you have chosen an instructor that fits your needs, be prepared to do what the instructor says and to learn what the instructor feels you require to achieve the goals you have in mind. Be open to taking in new information. You'll be glad you did.

When to Practice

Whenever you have a spare minute, even if it is only in fifteen-minute segments during the day or evening, use it to practice. Every moment you can spend at the instrument is worthwhile. No amount of time is too small, provided you keep going back to it whenever you have more time. There's nothing wrong with practicing at 11 P.M., 11 A.M., or whatever other time you can find, unless, of course, your neighbor or your spouse objects. If that happens, go get some earplugs (no, no—not for your spouse; for *you* so that you don't hear them yelling at you).

Ignoring Distractions

Do your best to avoid being distracted by telephone calls and other activities in your home when you practice. For however long you are at the instrument, try to put other things on hold. Perhaps you can arrange your schedule to practice when the baby is sleeping, when the telephone is quiet, when the children are at school, or when everyone else is already in bed. This may sound difficult, but if you can, it will assure better, more concentrated practice.

Playing for Others

If you enjoy playing for your friends, by all means do so. Playing for others offers you a chance to show off what you have learned and the progress you have made. It's a positive experience and generally makes students feel good about themselves. Conversely, don't force yourself to perform if it really makes you feel badly. However, sooner or later someone, someplace is going to have heard that you have been studying music and will want to hear you play. So it's good to get used to it, if you can. Besides, the more often you play for people, the easier it gets. Start out with baby steps; choose a very short piece, or play only a short part of a piece. Make sure you've practiced it a lot and are really confident about playing it for others. Try it out in front of one or two trusted family members a few times before playing for your friends ("in public"). Ask your family members to do everything they can to distract you while you're playing. (Doing that insures that when you play for your friends, their coughing or talking or moving around will not disturb you.)

Will you get nervous? Sure. Everybody does. So what? And what happens if you mess up? Well, there are two possibilities here: either the people you are playing for have a musical background or they don't. If they do, they will empathize with you and be encouraging and maybe even help you fix what you messed up. If they don't, you probably already know more about music than they do, and they won't even realize that you made a mistake. In any case, the first time you play for people is always the most difficult. After that it gets easier and easier. This is not a suggestion that you force yourself to play for others if it really makes you sick inside. However, if you possibly can, try it, at least once. You might surprise yourself and discover you really enjoy it.

Incidentally, musicians often complain of cold hands when they are about to play for someone. That's also part of being nervous (unless it is actually cold in the performance venue). Putting gloves or mittens on your hands for ten or fifteen minutes before you play warms up the hands and tricks the mind into feeling less nervous.

FOR INSTRUCTORS

Some of the questions parents and new adult students ask instructors are very difficult to answer. One of them is, "How long should I practice?" It's interesting that they never ask, "How long should I do homework?" To us, as instructors, the answer is simple: "As long as you have to" or "Until you learn it" or "As long as you can." Parents and new students don't always understand that.

They also ask, "How long will it take me to learn how to play well?" How often I wish we could tell them, "Who knows? Could be a year, two years, five years, maybe even more. It all depends on how efficiently you practice and how much you practice." New students and parents are looking for a more finite number.

Parents would never ask the principal in the elementary school where they are enrolling their pre-kindergarten child, "How long will my child have to be in school?" The true answer, "Seven hours a day, five days a week, forty-four weeks a year for at least twelve, but more likely sixteen, years," would probably make them stop and think about beginning their child's education. Consider an alternate response: "Learning music is a journey—a journey to a place you've never been before where you'll find new ideas, new culture, new food, new sights, new sounds, and new smells. Try to experience this new place with your whole being. Don't just see it. Feel it. Absorb everything you can, and then, when you must, go home. If you see your musical journey in that way, it will open your eyes to a whole new wonderful world for however long you decide to experience it. More-over, that journey will, forever, have a very positive effect on other areas of your life." This response won't exactly answer the questions mentioned above, but it is a response, perhaps, to questions that parents and new students have but don't yet know how to verbalize.

5

DELICATISSIMO

Little Things That Make a Big Difference

I learned that the only way you are going to get anywhere in life is to work hard at it. Whether you're a musician, a writer, an athlete, or a businessman, there is no getting around it. If you do, you'll win. If you don't, you won't.

—Bruce Jenner, Olympic gold medalist

PRELUDE

"Okay, Peter, let's look at your guitar-theory book now and check your homework," said Mr. Davis.

"Umm, it's right here, Mr. Davis . . . Uh, wait a minute. I know I put it in my bag . . . I'm sure I did. Huh! I thought I did . . . Um, it's not here. I guess I must have left it on the music stand at home."

"Peter, do you remember I told you to make a list of what to bring to every lesson? We discussed that several times. Did you make the list?"

"I forgot, Mr. Davis. I'm sorry. I've been very busy this week."

"But I wrote it in your notebook. Every day before you practice you *do* read your assignment, don't you?"

"Well, this week I didn't understand some stuff in the assignment, so I just practiced without looking at what you wrote. But I did practice."

"That's good, and I'm glad you practiced, but how could you know exactly what to do if you didn't see the assignment? It would have been better if you had called me on the phone and asked me about the assignment if you didn't understand it. In order to practice correctly you must always understand what I tell you to do in the book. It would have been perfectly all right for you to call me."

"I was busy, and I didn't want to bother you."

"It's no bother; I'd really rather you call me and ask me about whatever you don't understand."

"Oh, I dunno. I just figured that I'd wait until I saw you."

"So how did you practice that passage we had such a problem with last week? Do you remember that part? I wrote special instructions for how to practice it."

"I forgot about that. I guess I didn't practice that part at all . . ."

"Peter, if you don't do what I tell you to do in the assignment, how are you going to improve? And if you don't improve you're just going to get more and more frustrated and eventually you'll stop taking lessons."

"As a matter of fact, Mr. Davis, I wanted to talk to you about that. I don't think I've been making a lot of progress, and I've been thinking about stopping."

"Do you really want to stop lessons? You told me you loved music and wanted to learn."

"I do, but it's so frustrating. I just don't seem to be getting anywhere."

"But don't you understand that's because you don't always do what I tell you to do? I would like you to promise that this week you will really follow my instructions, in exactly the way I say. If you do, I'll make a promise to you that by next week you'll see a lot of improvement. Are you willing to do that?"

"Sure, Mr. Davis, but . . ."

"No but's; just do it, and let's see where you are next week. I bet you'll change your mind about stopping lessons."

"Okay; this week I'll do it your way. I'd like to see if it works."

FOR EVERYONE

Regardless of whether the student is a child or an adult, there are certain fundamental things besides an instrument that everyone must have in order to study music. These are: a notebook, a music manuscript book, and a recorder-player with blank discs. (Because you will need to carry music, a backpack, book bag, or tote bag of some kind is also a good idea, but wait to get these until after the first lesson.)

Making sure you arrive at the first lesson with these basic things enables you to take notes on what the instructor says. After all, you wouldn't go to a business meeting without a notebook, would you? Remember to turn on the recorder. The instructor is going to do a lot of talking in the first lesson and will ask a lot of questions in order to find out how much you or your child knows about music. Perhaps the instructor might even give a little written test (hence the music manuscript book). First lessons are used to help the instructor ascertain where to start with the student, much like a first day at school. During the first lesson you will learn what music books to get and perhaps which editions are preferred. A good instructor will discuss a roadmap or lesson plan with you—that is to say, the direction the lessons will take, what the student should expect, and what to expect from the student. There may be other instructions. Write everything down, or ask the instructor to write in the book.

Don't be surprised at the number of books the instructor will ask you to get. Ideally, a beginning student should have a theory book, an exercise or scale book, and at least three or four pieces to work on. These pieces may be in one or two books, or each one may be in a separate book. Having more than one piece to practice during the week provides musical variety, prevents boredom, and often offers instruction from different approaches or viewpoints.

At our institute each student brings to every lesson a notebook, manuscript book, theory book, scale book, exercises, recorder and discs, four or five music books, and flashcards. Regardless of whether you are learning to play a treble clef, bass clef, or alto/tenor clef instrument, all music students should learn the notes on at least two clefs.

If the instructor should, for any reason, indicate that he or she doesn't use original sheet music, just handouts and photocopies, this should be an immediate cause for concern. First of all, photocopying copyrighted material is, at the very least, immoral and unethical, and most of the time it is downright illegal. Photocopying is, in a sense, like stealing, even if it is a very short piece of music that you are copying. Composers who have done the work and publishers who have printed the music have a right to be paid for its use. Besides, individual sheets get lost, damaged, and shredded because students just don't take as much care of pieces of paper as they do of complete books. Therefore, if the instructor uses photocopies from the get-go, be wary.

Once you have received the list of music to be purchased, make sure you get all of it by the second, or at the very latest by the third, lesson. As I said in chapter four, because there are so many places to obtain music quickly these days, there is just no reason for putting off its purchase. Getting the music promptly starts the lessons off on a positive note.

FOR PARENTS

Make sure the child has a blank notebook in which the teacher can write all the assignments, corrections, and comments. This is the notebook from which *you* will read the assignments. Don't use it for anything besides the notes the teacher writes, and don't let the child write in it. In addition, the student should also have a music manuscript book. The instructor will ask the child to write musical notes and rhythms and other material in this book, so it is a very important part of the gear. And, of course, from the very first session remember to record every lesson in its entirety.

Making Lists

Make a list of all of the music books the student is working on. Put a number on each book and a corresponding number on the list. Using the list as reference, one by one, put the books into the book bag. Make sure all of them are packed in the book bag when the student goes to a lesson. When the student leaves, check that none of them are still sitting on the music stand. Any books left on the music stand are useless during the lesson. The teacher may or may not have copies of the pieces at the music studio. And even if there are copies there, the notes that the teacher has written in the music will be only on the student's copy.

Similarly, before the student leaves the lesson, use the list to ensure that all of the music books have been repacked and are available for practice at home. One of the most ingenious (and unnecessary) excuses for not being able to practice is "I left the music at Mr. So-and-so's house."

Of course, the opposite of this statement is "I really did practice that piece, Mr. So-and-so, but I just forgot the music at home." Checking to make sure all the books are in the book bag when they are supposed to be is a good way to circumvent such emergencies. The same goes for books that are going to school. If you have a list of everything that needs to be packed, the student will remember to pack them—that is, if he can remember where the list is. Along that line, you might want to tape the list to the outside of the book bag. (If that doesn't work try taping it to the student's forehead.)

On the same note (pun intended), make sure all the books come *out* of the book bag when the student practices at home. It is amazing how some books seem to get lost in the book bag. Students just seem to "forget" to take them out. As a result, they don't get practiced. Perhaps there is some big hole in the bottom of the book bag where some of the music just falls through and disappears. Then it magically reappears a couple of lessons later. And everybody wonders, "Huh! How did that happen?"

Checking the Assignment

As soon as possible after the lesson is over, look over the assignment. Make sure the child understands everything the teacher has written. If anything is unclear, call the instructor. If the instructor is unavailable, leave a message. Leave ten messages. Make sure the instructor calls back and unconfuses

you. Again, if too frequently the instructor claims to be too busy or too anything to return your call and clarify whatever is difficult to understand, then
get another instructor. You have a right to have all your questions answered
in a manner you can understand. Remember that the student cannot work
on, assimilate, or make use of what he does not understand.

Using the Assignment as a Recipe

During practice, use the instructions the teacher has written like a recipe.
Don't just read through the whole assignment and then put the book away.
Too many students try to read the assignments and then think they remember the corrections without looking at them. It's much better to read each
correction individually and then work on making that correction. After that
is accomplished, then read the next correction and work on that in the same
way. Of course, always make many, many repetitions of each correction.

Record the Practice

Encourage the student to record all practice. Take the disc and the machine to every lesson so that the teacher can spot-check the practice. Don't
just record "good" practices; record *all* practices. Ask the instructor to spot-
check the recording to see if the student is practicing the right way.

There's another reason for recording practice: the student can check
himself by listening to the disc. We cannot really hear ourselves when we
practice, first, because the brain colors our perception of our performance
and, second, because we are thinking of so many things while we are practicing. Sometimes we think we are playing or singing one way, yet when we
listen to the disc it sounds completely different. There are several ways to
record practice. Any of them are acceptable:

- record several practice sessions on one disc,
- use one disc for each practice session,
- put several pieces on one disc, or
- use one disc for each piece and keep adding practice sessions of that
  piece onto that disc.

Regardless of how you record the practice, make sure you keep track of
what dates you made the recordings and what pieces are on them. Put the
date on the label and number the disc so that you don't have to play the
disc to know what's on it.

Talk about the Lessons

Encourage the student to talk about the lessons and how he feels about the teacher. Don't ask the kind of questions that can be answered with one word, like "Do you like Mrs. Selmer?" Instead, ask open-ended questions, like "Why do you think Mrs. Selmer told you to keep your wrist up when you play 'The Golden Pond'?" If you get an, "I dunno" answer, write that down as one of the questions you will ask the teacher to explain.

Write a Journal

Encourage the student to write a journal about their feelings concerning the pieces they are working on. There are always particular passages that are difficult for students to learn. Ask the student to mark down those places in the journal, and discuss them with the instructor. If the child is too young to write, then you should do it. In any event, whatever is disturbing to the student should be brought up to the instructor in order to make those parts of the piece easier to learn and less frustrating. A journal is different from a scrapbook (see below) and should be kept separately.

Keep a Scrapbook

Help the student develop a scrapbook about the instruction. The scrapbook should contain the following information:

- the name of every piece over one minute long that the student has completed and that is considered a substantial piece of music,
- a photocopy of the finished piece,
- a CD or video tape of the finished piece,
- the date they began the piece,
- the date they finished the piece,
- the name of the piece,
- the name of the composer, with the dates of birth and death (though, of course, if the composer is still alive it would be really nasty to include a date of death),
- some information about the piece and the composer,
- information about how the student felt about the piece at the beginning and what their reaction was when it was finished,
- the venue where they performed it, if applicable,

- for whom they played it (including Uncle Jeffrey, Aunt Hilda, or even Sam, the dog),
- the audience reaction, and
- tickets and programs for each performance, if applicable, taped into the scrapbook.

This scrapbook helps students create a record of their progress. One or two years into lessons few students remember what they sounded like along the way. Even when we tell them, they still don't believe it. However, having a CD or a video recording, and seeing dates and a paragraph in their own hand about their feelings, gives them a barometer of their progress. That means more than all the pep talks in the world.

Point-Incentive Program

Rewards based on a point system also works well. Students earn points for

- playing pieces flawlessly the first time at a lesson,
- perfecting certain challenging exercises,
- learning scales at certain speeds,
- mastering a particular section of a piece that had been giving trouble for a long time,

and so on. The more difficult the challenge, the more points the student earns. The student, the parent, and the teacher put together a list of rewards that the student would like and assign a certain number of points to each. One reward might be a whole day out with the family, where the student calls the shots—what movie to see, where to go, where to eat—worth 200 points. Another might be a trip to a county fair, worth 500 points. A trip to Disney World might be worth 2,500 points, and so on.

Each student creates his own reward list, and the teacher and parent assign the number of points necessary to earning the reward. The teacher should enter the earned points into the student's stamp book, and when the stamp book contains the number of points needed for a particular treat, the student turns the book in and redeems the prize. The object of the point system is to set goals at different levels requiring varying amounts of work from the student. The point system goes a long way toward encouraging the student to continually improve.

Of course, when the child turns in the stamp book to redeem the prize, mom and dad had better be ready to make good on the promise. No fair copping out on your side of the bargain after the child has worked so hard to get the prize.

Earning Diplomas

Students should earn "diplomas," certificates, or some sort of recognition whenever they pass from one level to another.

Blowing Off Steam

There will be many moments when the student becomes tense and up-tight. Perhaps he can't make his fingers do something; he keeps making the same mistake, or the finger keeps missing a note. You may have noticed that many children throw things when they become frustrated. (Adults might not throw things, but practice often makes them feel like it.) I know that some parents will object to this idea, but here is a positive way to channel that urge. Teach the child to throw the music book on the floor, hard, when upset! Then have him pick it up. Throw it again, and pick it up again. Let the child do this several times. Eventually, the child begins to recognize

how funny it is to throw the music, especially when he has to pick it up again. The secret to this exercise is to pick the book up one more time than throwing it down. That rids the body of frustration and allows the student to try again. Don't laugh! Of course this exercise is only for music practice. Otherwise you may find household objects flying from angry hands onto the floor all day.

For those who don't like the idea of throwing a book, here's an alternative: Ask the student to run to the end of the room or hall. If there isn't a hall, ask the student to do a somersault. Ask him to repeat that motion several times. Guaranteed, the student will soon feel better, and maybe both of you will have a laugh.

Practicing in Costume

Let a young child practice in costume. Choose a costume that the child particularly likes, and only use it during practice. That's the "practice costume." Why not? Little girls who study dance have those cute pink tutus, and the boys have the handsome black tights. (Do they call them one-ones?) Why shouldn't music students have the same fun? However, make sure the costume is comfortable. It can't be itchy, make the child hot, hang down over the hands, or obstruct vision. And the costume must be durable, at least enough to survive one or two washings.

Practice Buddies

If it's possible, find practice buddies for the student. If you or the child knows other children who have studied with the same instructor or learned the same music, having the child talk to them about problem passages in the piece can be helpful. A conversation with a study buddy might go like this:

TIMMY: I just can't learn that part. I always mess it up right here. I don't know why. It's just so hard. You must have had trouble with this piece also, Tommy. How did you fix it?

TOMMY: Sure, I did it wrong in the beginning, too, and it gave me a lot of trouble. But then after I practiced it in teeny parts for a few days it got easier. I had to do it really slow, but I finally got it.

TIMMY: Can you show me how you practiced it?

TOMMY: Sure. Watch; this is what I did. [Performs passage] Here—you try it.

TIMMY: [Trying it Tommy's way] "You're right, Tommy. It's a little easier this way. I'll work on it like this at home. Thanks for the help.

Study buddies can help students feel less irritated when they have problems learning something. The sense of "Been there, done that, got past it and succeeded" rubs off and makes the child feel better and helps him realize that the problem is fixable and isn't permanent.

FOR STUDENTS

Everything written above to help parents aid their children's practice is just as applicable for adults (except maybe the costume idea; but, then again, you might find a costume you like and want to wear it, in which case, go for it!).

The Basic Gear

Start out with a blank notebook, manuscript book, and recording device. The manuscript book may stay empty for a while, but there *will* come a moment when the instructor decides to write some musical examples for you and will say, "By the way, do you have a music manuscript book?" Won't you feel good when you can answer, "Yes, of course; here it is"?

Getting the Materials

I've spoken several times about getting the music an instructor wants you to have, but it cannot be stressed too much. When the instructor gives you the names of books or pieces to obtain, get them as soon as you can.

Don't Ask, Don't Borrow

Never, never, ever ask the instructor to get material for you. You wouldn't ask your doctor to pick up your medicine from the pharmacy, would you? And you certainly wouldn't ask your college professor to run to the bookstore and purchase your textbooks. As a matter of fact, you wouldn't even ask your mail delivery person to wrap your package for you. Instructors are professionals. They are there to teach. They are not delivery people, they are not servants, they are not valets, and they are not your assistants. Even though you may have a carload of people to do your errands at your office or home, never ask for that kind of service from the instructor. On the other hand, you could ask someone from the carload to buy your music for you.

Along the same line, don't ask to borrow material from the teacher. Not for a day, not for an hour, not for a minute. If the teacher shows you something that you find particularly interesting or even irresistible, go out and get it for yourself.

The Assignment

Remember to check the assignment and make sure you understand everything in it. Just spend a few minutes when you get home and look it over. It shouldn't take more than five minutes.

Using the assignment as a recipe is really easy for an adult—perhaps easier than it is for a child. Just put your assignment book right next to you when you practice, and take each item, each correction, and practice that part isolated from the rest of the piece until you can do it correctly and easily several times. Then go to the next item on the list. Fix that one. In like fashion, go down the list with each correction the instructor has made. We'll talk more about this in later chapters, but, for now, remember to keep the assignment near to you and to work from it. Don't just read it once and put it away.

Record the Practice

Recording the practice is great for students. It's a way of checking ourselves and finding out what we really sound like. Fortunately (or maybe unfortunately), the recorder doesn't lie. "Ooh, did I really get so much faster?" The recorder says, Yes, you did. "My goodness; I didn't know I left that measure out." The recorder says you did. If you had played it, it would have been on the disc. "Wow, it sounds so choppy. I couldn't have played it like that." The recorder says you did. If you had played it smoothly, it would have sounded smooth on the disc.

Another reason for recording the practice is to let the instructor spot check what you do at home. When the teacher hears the disc and fast forwards and stops, fast forwards and stops, he has an opportunity to listen to the quality of the practice at home. It's almost as if the instructor were sitting by your side during practice.

Write a Journal

Writing a journal is just as valuable for an adult student as for a younger person. Keep a record of the musical passages that trouble you and present them to the instructor so that he can offer suggestions about how to solve the problems. You could even color code the problems in the journal: blue for rhythm, red for notes, yellow for dynamics, orange for phrasing, and so on. Put a matching little dot in the music in the same color (with a pencil that is erasable) so that when you talk with the instructor about the problems you immediately know what the problem was at a glance. It saves time. Remember, most lessons are one hour long, and that time flies.

Keep a Scrapbook

The scrapbook idea is really important. Students never realize the progress they have made, and six months or a year down the road it helps a lot to have some way of measuring how far you've come.

Point-Incentive Program

Adults often think the point program is silly, but what's wrong with rewarding yourself when you have finished a project or when you have mastered a real challenge? Okay, so maybe your idea of a reward isn't Disney World, but surely there's something out there that you have been wanting for some time that could be used to pat yourself on the back and recognize a job well done.

Make a List of Breakthroughs

Making a list of breakthroughs—musical issues you have successfully resolved—goes right in step with rewarding yourself for finishing projects and mastering challenges. Along your musical journey you will encounter and solve many problems. Keeping a list of these will remind you of what you *can* do and what you have *already* done. As the list of accomplishments grows, so will your self-confidence and self-esteem.

Blowing Off Steam

Book-throwing therapy is beneficial to adult students, too. No matter how silly you think it is, just do it! I guarantee it'll make you laugh; you'll feel better and you'll return to the practice with renewed energy, a happier spirit, and a smile on your face. And what's wrong with that? Absolutely nothing! Come on, try it; it's fun! Pick the music up, and throw it on the floor. Pick it up again. Throw it on the floor again, harder. Pick it up again. Throw it much harder. Pick it up again. Throw it even harder. Pick it up again. Give it your best throw, really hard. Come on, now. Tell the truth. Don't you feel better? Now, stop laughing, pick up the music, put it on your music stand, and try again. This time it will be better. I promise.

FOR INSTRUCTORS

In the eyes of the parents and the student the instructor is always the expert. That means the student's family looks to the teacher to tell them what to do, what to get, how to do it or get it, how much to pay for it, and where to go to do it or get it. Instructors are there to teach, to guide, to advise, to inspire. It is never, ever the job of the teacher to *do it for or instead of* the student.

The instructor should check out the instrument the student brings to lessons from time to time to make sure it is in good working order. If something needs fixing, it *is* part of the job of the instructor to tell the student or the parent what's wrong with it and where to go to get it fixed. It is *not* the job of the instructor to fix the instrument, unless the repair job is so simple and fast that it can be done during the lesson while the student is present. Repairs that are easy—maybe putting a new string on a guitar or greasing a wind instrument—are fixable in moments and can be done by the instructor. Anything requiring more should be redirected to a trusted repair person.

If the instructor teaches at his own studio, the environment should be comfortably warm or cool. It should be inviting and as conducive to playing as possible, with plenty of light and air. If the instructor goes to the home of a student and the place where the student has his instrument makes teaching or practice difficult, the instructor should discuss whatever adjustments need to be made with the responsible parent. (If the instructor goes to the student's home, that's also a good time to check out the instrument.)

The instructor should never, ever lend anything to the student. This may sound mean, but lending something to a student is the fastest way to insure that the student

- has a sudden family emergency and must fly to Australia immediately,
- has a sudden family emergency and must fly to the moon immediately,
- has a family emergency where the house burns down and all the possessions of the family (and anything borrowed from the teacher) have been destroyed by the fire, or
- never shows up at a lesson again.

The instructor should *never* buy music or anything else for the student, even if the instructor is already in the music store and has the objects in hand.

However, if, while at the store, the instructor finds something that would be useful for the student, it would be helpful to make a note of the item—the ISBN number (if it is a book) or the item number—and pass the information on to the student at the next lesson or with a quick phone call. Then, of course, it must be up to the student to go and get the item.

As instructors we must always try to be at the top of our teaching form. Most of us are, but sometimes, after we have been in front of students or classes a long time, we can fall into a rut and get into a "same old, same old" grind. Instead of seeing the world with the newborn enthusiasm of the student, we look at life through tired, worn-out, "been there, done that" eyes. When that happens, it is important to re-energize ourselves. Take a class. Learn something about the new technology. See what's out there that wasn't out there a month ago. In order to keep our students interested and motivated, we must always be at the top of our form. And we must do whatever it takes to get us there. Students are in the world of today and tomorrow. If we are still in the world of yesterday, or sick and tired of the world of today, and a little afraid of the world of tomorrow, we can be of little help to them. We must be the best that we can be in order to help our students be the best that *they* can be.

6

POCO AGITATO

Things You Should Never Do

Music is nothing separate from me. It *is* me—you'd have to remove the music surgically.

—Ray Charles, musician

PRELUDE

"Go practice *now*, Teresa. You've been puttering around all day. Quit your procrastinating, and go do it. *Now*," says Mrs. Collins, clearly irritated.

Stomping her foot, Teresa answers, "I don't feel like practicing now, Mom. I'll do it later."

"Why do I always have to tell you to practice, Teresa? Why does your music always cause a battle around here? I shouldn't have to be responsible for your practice. They're your lessons, after all. I feel like I always have to push you when it's time for you to go practice."

Getting angrier and angrier, Teresa yells, "You're right, Mom; it's my practice, and I hate it. It's boring, and it takes forever to learn anything. You ought to try it and see how it feels. Then you'd know why I hate it. Leave me alone. I just don't feel like doing it now. I'll do it later. Maybe!"

Mrs. Collins yells even louder. "No, you'll do it *right now*, or you're not going to Disney World. And, what's more, I'll make you practice all Saturday and Sunday. You won't go anywhere the whole weekend. You better get in there right now and practice for an hour. Go on! I'm going to time you. I don't want to see your face until the hour is up."

"That's just fine with me. I don't want to see your face either or the teacher's face either, ever again. I hate practicing, I hate music, I hate the teacher, and I hate you." Teresa turns to storm away.

"I don't care. Go in and practice for an hour *right now*. If you keep arguing, I'll make it two hours. And I'm going to call the teacher and tell him exactly how you behave when it's time to practice."

"Fine. And make sure you tell him I hate music and want to stop my lessons!"

FOR EVERYONE

So far, I've said a lot about how to approach practice in a more positive manner. Equally important are those things a parent, a student, or even an instructor must *never* do.

FOR PARENTS

Don't Time the Practice

Never tell a student to "go practice for an hour." Thinking about how long to practice means thinking about time, not practice. It's much more important to think about the quality of the practice, rather than the amount of time. If possible, as I suggested in chapter 4, remove the clocks in the room when the student practices. When the student discovers that, "Wow, I can do this," he feels good about practicing—like he is on a roll—and is willing to keep at it longer. This success creates an incentive to try harder and work longer. Practice doesn't "make perfect," but it sure helps make what you are doing better!

Never tell a student to "Go back and practice some more. You aren't finished, yet. You have another fifteen minutes [or however many more] to go." Again, that's timing the practice. It won't take long for the child to begin watching the clock to see how much longer the prescribed amount of practice time is. The idea is to encourage *good* practice, not to prolong *bad* practice. A student has "finished practicing" when all the corrections have been systematically worked on in order to improve them and fix what is wrong. Practicing a long time without benefit has no value.

Break Up the Practice

It is usually not necessary for a student to do all the day's practice in one sitting. If the child practices at home, even if only in ten-, fifteen-, or twenty-minute increments, as long as she goes back to it several times a day, the time adds up. However, remember to think quality, not quantity. If the quality of practice is good, obviously the more the student practices (regardless of how long each sitting lasts), the more progress she will make. We all have commitments during the day—school, job, family, extracurricular activities. But there are usually breaks between. If you can help the child find a segment of time in the morning to practice before the busy day begins, another segment in the late afternoon, and perhaps, through good planning, and a little luck, another bit at night, go for it! It is especially important to decide beforehand what should be worked on in the time allotted in order to derive the most benefit from the practice.

Don't Threaten, Don't Bribe

Never force a student to practice. Encourage—firmly, but gently. Often, taking the student to a concert where she can hear pieces she is working on played by professional musicians inspires her to new efforts, especially a concert where her own instructor or children her own age are playing.

Don't be concerned if a child goes through periods when she will not practice. This is common, and it passes. Don't panic. Try asking the student to create something musical for you. "Can you make up a happy piece for me, Joey?" often helps. After the student has created a piece of music, consider one of the following:

- Say, "Oh, that was so pretty; it sounds a little like the piece you were practicing, doesn't it? Let's listen to both of them. Play the piece you wrote, and play the piece you were learning. Let's see if they sound different."
- Or you could ask the child to try to write out what she played.
- Or ask the student to practice rhythms, instead of playing the instrument, or to try playing the piece on the table (that's really "tabling" the problem, isn't it?).

Never threaten a student with the loss of something he wants if he does not do as well as you think he should or practice as long as you'd like. Never say, "If you don't do better in your music studies, you'll be grounded for a month." That's the quickest way to make a student hate music.

Never use music instruction as a weapon against school work or anything else the student does. "If your grades don't improve, I'll stop your music lessons." "If you don't stop staying out so late, I'll stop your music lessons." "If you don't stop using drugs, I'll stop your music lessons." It is just a hop, skip, and a jump from that threat to the student's saying to her parent, "Fine; I never wanted them anyway. I hate music lessons. I hate the teacher, and I hate you!" We want music to be a positive experience. Don't cause the student to think of music as a weapon to be used against her.

Never use practice as punishment: "If you don't do your homework right now, I'll make you practice two extra hours, and I'll make you practice all weekend, and you won't be able to go out with your friends." Practicing is hard, it's lonely, it's boring, and it's tedious. Don't add to the problem by using it as a threat. Any interest the student has in learning the instrument will be destroyed by such threats. Rather, encourage the child to do more because the results are so wonderful; the fact is, they really are.

Never tell the student that if he practices all week he won't have to practice on the weekend. That's like telling someone that if she eats all his lunch today he won't have to eat tomorrow. Not eating is detrimental to the body. Not practicing is detrimental to the student's progress.

Never bribe a child to practice. I know of one case where a mother began to give her child a dollar for every day that he practiced. Soon, the child began asking for two dollars and then three. Little by little, the child realized that even if he only practiced a few days a week, he could make a pile of money. Eventually, the money became much more important to him than the musical rewards of practicing.

Don't Mock or Compare

Never insist that your child perform for friends or family if the child doesn't like playing in front of others. If she *does* decide to play for family or friends, never ridicule or make fun of the child's mistakes, not even in private. Always be encouraging, positive, and upbeat.

Never compare the child's performance to someone else's performance, not even privately to yourself. There will always be someone who plays better than the student and someone who doesn't play as well. Let the student compete only with herself and try to be the best that she can be.

Never apologize to others for a child who gives a weak performance—not in front of the child, and certainly not behind her back.

Taking Responsibility

Never allow the student to blame you for what she hasn't done. What the student didn't, can't, or won't do is *not your fault*. Rather, it is the student's responsibility to practice, to pack the music, to carry the music, to show up at lessons, and to advance to the next level. Help the child learn to *take* that responsibility early on. Never let the child say, "I don't have the music, because my mother didn't pack it in my book bag." From the beginning, make the student understand that it is *her* job to pack the book bag, and, if necessary, teach her how. If the child tells her instructor, "I didn't work on that part because my father forgot to tell me," remind her to listen to the disc of the lesson (remember the discussion about recording the lessons earlier?). Students also might say, "I practiced it that way because my sister told me to"; but the sister isn't the student, as you will remind her. The best excuse (and I'm sure you've heard this one) is, "I couldn't practice because the dog ate my music." (Maybe the dog is a critic.)

When Nerves Take Over

Even a student who really knows the piece well sometimes panics and flounders when playing it in front of people. It's called "being nervous." We've all suffered through the jitters at one time or another, haven't we? Oh, the stories I could tell you about what nerves can do. Here's just one of them:

Jose, a voice student, had quite a nice voice and looked forward to singing at the semiannual student recital. He knew the songs he was to sing inside and out. When his name was called, he walked to the stage with confidence. Front and center, he bowed to the audience and then nodded to the pianist to begin. The introduction to the song was long, about ten or twelve seconds. In that space of time, his mind blanked out, his nerves took over, and when he opened his mouth to sing, there was . . . nothing. Not a sound, not a peep. The pianist stopped, went back to the beginning of the piece, and started again. Once more, when the moment came for him to sing, Jose couldn't make a sound. He began to tremble. It was quite noticeable. I walked to the stage, took the microphone from his hands and talked to the audience about the wonderful progress Jose had made in the time he had been studying. I mentioned his expanding repertoire and his being offered a solo in his church. Then, I explained that what the audience was witnessing was a bad case of nerves. "And," I added, "if any of you thinks it's easy to come up here and perform, you are welcome to take the stage." Needless to say, no one took me up on my offer, but by the time I finished talking, Jose had regained his composure and sang two beautiful solos without a hitch.

Parental Supervision

Don't leave a young student to practice without supervision. The child will feel better if you are there, and, probably, so will you. Being in the room where the student practices means you can better control how long the child practices and how well. In addition, you can recognize when to change activities if you are present. Come to think of it, don't leave a young child without supervision, period—not in the practice room, and not any-where else, either.

A Home, Not a Battlefield

Never make the practice room a battlefield. If you are a supervising par-ent, never yell at a student because you think she is practicing badly. Never call the student names when she can't make her hands (and her brain) do something, and never, ever curse at the student during practice. (It's not a terrific idea to curse at her at other times, either!)

Similarly, if you are the supervising parent, never allow the child to yell at you or curse at you.

Praise, Praise, Praise

Never ignore a child if she asks you to "Listen to what I can do." Stop whatever you are doing, and listen. Regardless of what you think it sounds like, clap, whistle, screech, yell hooray, jump up and down, and in every other way you can think of be enthusiastic and encouraging. Tell her that her playing is terrific. Make the child feel good. After a lot of effort, she has finally achieved what she has worked so hard for and feels good about it. This is *wonderful*. Remember, you are the mirror by which the student judges her own progress. The child is excited and proud of what she has accomplished, and you must be equally if not *more* excited. If you do not show immediate and enthusiastic approval, you will crush the student's feeling of success.

Be sure to offer increased enthusiasm and emotional support as the assignments get harder. As the student passes each level, the complexity of each assignment increases, and so does the amount of time needed to get to the next level. Frustration heightens. Usually the problem is just one of patience and perseverance. Encourage the student to keep at it!

Professional Musicians, Beware

If you are a musician, never try to teach your own child, as your method is probably very different from the instructor's. Don't give the student tips that you may have gotten when you were a student, as they may be in direct conflict with what the instructor is teaching. However, do reinforce whatever the teacher has written in the assignment.

Another reason for not teaching your own child is that the child doesn't recognize you as "teacher." She thinks of you as Mommy or Daddy, and a parent-child relationship is completely different from that of teacher-student. When the teacher is a family member, the student feels free to argue or direct the course of the lesson. This creates battles, debates, and arguments and erodes the teacher-student relationship. Consider that a doctor seldom treats her own family members.

Don't Offer Crutches

Never write English letters into the music or on the instrument to help the child remember the notes. The student must learn to recognize the music notes in the language of music, without crutches to help her along. The crutches actually make the learning take longer.

As an example, if you are looking for the men's bathroom in a Hispanic restaurant and you don't speak Spanish, ask yourself which you will recognize first, a sign that reads "Hombres" or a sign that reads "Men." Students always gravitate toward the familiar first. If we write English letters to help the student learn the notes, the student's brain will notice the English letters first and may not even *see* the note above the English letter. If, on the other hand, the student forces the eyes to recognize the notes on the instrument and in the music without such aides, she will actually learn them faster.

Watch for Signs

Never ignore the student's reactions at home. If you notice that the student has begun to lose interest in music, discuss it with the teacher immediately so that together you can reenergize the student. Sometimes the answer is changing the style of teaching, the style of music, the instrument, or even the teacher. With a new style of music, a new way of teaching, or even a new instrument the student's interest often renews and he does very well. Don't let problems escalate. Deal with them as soon as possible.

A Few Final Don'ts

A note of caution to parents: don't allow a child to change instruments too frequently or too soon. The natural reaction of a child who doesn't like practice (and none of us does) is to say "I hate piano" or "I can't stand guitar" or "I don't like clarinet; I don't want to do it anymore!" This often happens after the first or second month of lessons, when the novelty has worn off, the work has begun, and frustration has reared its ugly head. If the child keeps changing instruments, he never gets to work at any of them long enough to find out which one he really likes. The student should study an instrument until he can play, at the very least, a few pieces reasonably well before trying something else, ideally for at least six months and certainly not less than four.

Don't offer misplaced sympathy for a student. A young, frustrated child will often try to make the parent (or whoever else will listen) feel sorry for her and rescue her from this torturous activity called practice. "Oh," she might say to her mother after the second or third lesson, with tears in her eyes, "the violin is so heavy. I can't hold it. The strings hurt my fingers." Mommy's immediate reaction is to think about terminating the lessons because the poor child is in such pain. Give me a break! In that kind of scenario, the instrument that the child is *really* playing is not the violin—it's the *parent*! Don't fall for it! Instead of offering to terminate the lessons, encourage the child to try a little harder. Music, driving a race car, sky diving, skating, swimming (the list goes on and on), and any other activity that involves mental and physical coordination requires work. Performed well, these activities become skills. Performed with a little bit of magic, they become art. Regardless of the level to which we develop these skills, the one thing they all require is the discipline of practice.

FOR STUDENTS

Making Progress

Don't get discouraged if you seem to not be making any progress even though you practice every day. If you are practicing conscientiously, it will get better. Just keep at it. Progress doesn't happen at a constant rate but often comes in spurts. You may not see any difference for a few weeks, and then, one day, almost magically, the problem you thought you had isn't there any longer. The trick is to keep at it even when you don't see improvement and to try to practice as consistently and as productively as possible. Make a little sign to put on your music stand: "Most musical problems can be solved if students practice smaller sections, practice longer, practice slower, and make more repetitions."

Dealing with Frustration

Don't try to ignore frustration. Sometimes even adult students need to let off steam. It's okay. Go ahead. Cuss at the music. Yell at your fingers.

Jump up and down. Scream and stomp your feet if you need to. However, you might want to check around to make sure no one is in earshot when you begin your tirade, and just remember that when you are finished you ought to go back to practicing.

Adult Nerves

Don't be upset when you get nervous. Notice that I said "when," and not "if." Adults and older students usually get more nervous than children. Children are natural hams. They love to show off what they can do, even if they don't always do it perfectly. They generally don't get rattled quite the way adults do, because they don't possess the capacity for embarrassment that comes with age and experience. The important thing to remember is that, regardless of age, when you are a student you are just *beginning*. No one should compare you to a seasoned performer, and if anyone does, they are wrong, not you. After all, they aren't paying for tickets to your concert, are they? So try to relax as much as possible, and if the butterflies continue to flutter inside your belly, invite them for lunch.

Don't Give Up

Don't think your music-learning experience will go smoothly. It won't. Don't expect it to. Irritations crop up. Emergencies arise. Accidents occur. Impatience builds up. Life happens. Don't give up. Ultimately the things that bother you the most will resolve themselves, and you'll be so glad that you stuck with the inner pleasure that music brings.

FOR INSTRUCTORS

Breaking Up Practice

Although it may seem more productive for the student to practice in one longer session, suggesting the option of breaking up the practice may make it easier on the student, especially if attention span or other considerations are to be taken into account. Try to get the student and the parents to focus on the quality, not quantity, of practice.

Help Family Members Focus on the Positive

Instructors must always try to help students and parents focus on the positive and defuse, in advance wherever possible, any situations that could potentially cause problems. Encourage the student or parent to call you or e-mail you with questions or problems. Even though it impinges on your personal time, it will help keep the student interested and motivated. There's nothing quite like having parents say to their friends, "My child has a great instructor who is always available to answer our questions and solve any musical problems we might have."

In addition, at the lesson, without getting into long-winded conversations that delay the start of the teaching hour, it's very important to ask enough questions about what is going on at home to ensure that there are no negative issues cropping up that could influence or sabotage the student's practice.

If you suspect that a frustrated parent (or student) is using any of the *don'ts* I have mentioned in this chapter to control practice, it's very important to nip them in the bud. Try to offer creative, positive alternatives to counter anything negative going on at home. If you hear that a student is being bribed to practice, suggest instead the incentive program, which teaches the student goal-setting skills. If you think a student is not taking enough responsibility for her music studies, make sure you hand the packed book bag to the student and not to the parent at the end of a lesson. If a parent compares the child's progress to that of someone else, remind the parent how individual each student is and how important it is to revel in that individuality.

But I Played It Perfectly at Home . . .

When students make a mistake during a lesson, they often complain, "I don't understand why I'm messing up here. I played it perfectly at home." (How many times have you heard *that* comment?) Sometimes, in our haste to continue with the lesson and avoid too much conversation, we let a comment like that slide by without answering. We shouldn't. The student that makes that complaint is really frustrated and deserves a response. Tell her that there are three possibilities for the mistakes during the lesson:

- maybe it was only after having played it imperfectly many times at home that they finally played it once correctly;
- maybe they didn't play it as perfectly as they thought they did in the first place;
- or maybe it's just those butterflies again.

Whatever the reason, the students deserve a compassionate answer, and we must do our best to provide one.

A *good* doctor listens with an open ear and an open mind to the complaints of the patient. We, too, must listen to our students and their parents and, based at least partly on what they tell us, make suggestions that will help them derive the greatest benefit and the most enjoyment from their musical instruction.

7

L'ISTESSO TEMPO

What to Think about First

Music takes a lot of devotion and work—or maybe I should say *play*—
because if you love it, that's what it amounts to. I haven't found any
shortcuts, and I've been looking for a long time.

—Chet Atkins, guitarist

PRELUDE

"Travis just doesn't want to continue his lessons. He says he hates practicing. He tells me that he can't stand having to stay upstairs all alone in his
room for an hour in order to practice. He complains that it is lonely."

"He's right; it is. Can't you stay in the room with him when he practices?
That way he'd have company. And you'd be able to monitor what he does
and make sure he is practicing according to the instructions I write in his
assignment book."

"I can't do that; I have things to do. I don't have the time to be sitting
with him. He has to do his own practicing. It's his responsibility."

"But he's only seven."

"That's okay—he has other chores he has to do, and he manages to do
them by himself. He helps set the table, he puts the dishes in the sink after dinner, he helps take the garbage out, and he even combs his hair by
himself."

"But those are all things that only take a few minutes to do. He doesn't have to sit by himself for a long period of time."

"Well, most of the time he also does his homework by himself. He only comes to me if he needs help."

"How about having him practice at times when you can be with him? He'll do a better job of practicing if you are there."

"I have other children. I have so many things to do when I come home from work: cooking, laundry, helping with homework, shopping, cleaning up, making sure everyone takes a shower, getting lunches ready for school, grading papers, getting myself ready for work the next day."

"How about having Travis break up his practice into several smaller time segments? Remember we talked about that? It would make it easier on him, and maybe you would be able to stay with him at least some of the time."

"No, I just don't have the time to sit with him. There are just not enough hours in the day. Besides, Travis knows that I listen from downstairs while I'm doing things. And I call up to him if I hear him stop playing. From time to time, I even go upstairs and step into his room to see how he is doing. As a matter of fact, that's exactly how I found out that he was playing ball in his room when he was supposed to be practicing. Can you beat that? He was playing ball when he was supposed to be practicing. If I hadn't gone up there, I would never have known."

"Playing ball? What do you mean? How is that possible? Either he was up there practicing or he wasn't."

"I heard him playing through the piece a whole lot of times. It sounded great, so I went upstairs and opened his door to watch him. I had planned to tell him how good it was. There he was, throwing a ball up against the wall, and he had a CD playing his piece. He just kept replaying the CD so I'd think that he was practicing. Until I came into his room I couldn't know that. When I asked him why he wasn't practicing, he told me that he hated practicing, and this way he found a way for someone else to do it for him."

FOR EVERYONE

What people hate about practice is the length of time it takes to learn anything, how many times a piece has to be repeated before it is finally and forever learned, and how boring those repetitions are. Everyone would like to be able to learn whatever the assignment is in a half hour or so and be able to play it perfectly forevermore. Wishful thinking! It's not going to happen. However, there are many things everyone can do to derive the greatest benefit from the practice in the shortest period of time. Everything a student does at the instrument affects the practice and how fast he learns:

- the way the student sits at the instrument,
- how much stress the student feels (from outside responsibilities) when he sits down to practice,
- how long the student practices, and
- how much of that practice is purposeful, well-organized work and how much is just mindless repetition.

The more organized and uniform the practice is, the more productive it will be. Therefore, from the very beginning, students should develop good learning habits so that they won't have to fix things later that they should have learned right in the first place. Developing good habits right from the beginning enables students to triple productivity while keeping boredom to a minimum.

FOR PARENTS

How to Sit

Regardless of age, from the first time a student sits down to practice, the body position should be as correct as possible. The height of the seat and the distance from the music is very important to comfortable, productive practice, because if the body position is incorrect, it is more difficult to play the instrument. Don't allow the child to sit in a wrong position with the expectation of fixing it later. That is a waste of valuable learning time.

Each instrument is a little different in terms of how high or low the student must sit, how the student must hold the instrument, and what position the body must be in. Some instruments, like an acoustic bass and the pipe organ, require students to sit on seats that are quite high because the instruments are big and cumbersome and the student must be able to reach all the parts. (Since parents of young children aren't going to have to worry about their six, seven, or eight year old playing the acoustic bass or the pipe organ, let's leave those instruments alone for now.)

In some cases students must sit to the side of an instrument or hold the instrument to the side of where they're sitting. In any event, students must be able to sit comfortably, close enough to the instrument to play it, and close enough to the music to be able to see it easily. Students mustn't slouch when they are playing an instrument because it affects the distance that they are from the music and the way they play. (They shouldn't slouch any other time, either.) Children tend to slouch more than adults do, so parents need to be especially diligent in encouraging the young student to sit up straight.

The chair on which the child sits when practicing should not have arms (you can have arms, and your chair can have arms, but the child's chair shouldn't—and it probably shouldn't have hands or feet, either). An alternative to a chair is a bench, preferably one that is adjustable. Adjustable benches are available at many music stores, are relatively inexpensive, and are just as comfortable as regular chairs. Besides, they accommodate any student, regardless of size, age, or growth spurts.

The child should sit sufficiently forward on the chair so that his back doesn't touch the back of the chair and his feet are planted firmly on the floor. If his feet don't reach the floor, consider placing them on a box to prevent dangling.

Again, it is important that the child learns the correct way to sit as soon after beginning lessons as possible. After you have established where the child should place the chair, the music stand, the feet, and the body parts, consider putting marks on the floor and on the chair so that you and the child don't have to rediscover the correct position each time the child practices.

Relaxing the Body

To minimize stress, be conscious of relaxing the muscles, the body, and the mind. When students' bones and muscles become stressed, everything else tightens up. The child must learn to breathe normally and swallow. It may sound funny, but students who are really wound up sometimes forget to swallow. And I have seen students become so tense while playing that little by little their shoulders crept up to their ears. When I reminded them to relax, their shoulders dropped three or four inches. If you ever notice that your child's shoulders are tensed and near the side of his face, stop and make the child consciously relax.

Make sure there is enough light in the room for good vision. The child should be able to see the music clearly and easily from where he is sitting. The distance from the seat to the music stand is not easy to define: it's somewhere in between far and near. It's not as far as the child has to look when reading street signs, and it's not as close as when reading a book. Sometimes students have a little trouble adjusting to this in-between position, but with a little practice (there's that word again) the eyes adapt.

If the child consistently has trouble seeing the music from where he is sitting, and you are certain that the distance is correct, consider having his eyes checked by a health professional.

Preparing the Mind

Encourage the child to clear his mind of stress during practice. Choose a time that is relatively calm, and try to keep interference at a minimum. Create some kind of ritual that helps the child relax and mentally prepares him for practice. Some people sit with their instruments in hand and close their eyes for a few moments. Some shake their heads and shrug their shoulders. Find out what works for your child, and have him do that same motion at the beginning of each practice session.

How Much to Practice

The more a child can practice, the better the result. However, whether that practice is done in one lump or spread out during the course of a day is really not important. The quality of practice is what is important. If the practice is purposeful and well organized, the child will derive the very best results from it, even if he doesn't practice as much as the parent would like.

Learning Music Notation

Students, regardless of age, should learn music notation as soon as possible. Forget all the horror stories you've heard about learning to read music. They are just plain nonsense. There is absolutely no reason for struggling. Students should learn music notation with a five-pronged approach:

- flashcards,
- hand staff,
- note recognition,
- direction of the notes, and
- eyes front, heads up.

Flashcards   At our institute, students use 5" × 7" flashcards, which are suitable for children or adults. The cards cover a range of notes four octaves long, which is a little longer than the range of any instrument except keyboards and harp. On the front side of the card is a staff, a clef sign, and a note. On the back is the answer.

Here's how to work with flashcards effectively: Use the buddy system to learn the notes. The buddy holds each card with the note facing the student and the answer facing the buddy. Because the answer is seen by the buddy, the buddy doesn't need to know anything about music to help. He just has to read the answer and make sure that is what the student says.

The student must use the following drill, always saying the same words in the same order:

- say the clef sign (e.g., treble clef);
- say the placement of the note (e.g., space four);
- say the name of the note (e.g., E); and
- play the note in the correct place on the instrument.

When the student can identify all the notes in the flashcard range, reduce the flashcards by 50 percent. Then the student should learn them again in the smaller size. Keep reducing the size of the flashcards by 50 percent until they are smaller than the notes in the music. Each time the student adapts to the smaller size, he must also speed up his responses. Ultimately, the student must learn to say and play each note within less than two seconds.

Hand Staff   Turn the child's right hand sideways at eye level so that the child is looking at the back of his hand. If the child's head is north and the feet are south, then his right-hand fingertips will be west (left), and the

wrist will be east (right). In this position, spread out his fingers so that they and the spaces between them look like the lines and spaces of one staff. Make sure the thumb is the lowest finger and the pinky is the highest.

On the fingers of the right hand, ask the child to say the lines of the treble clef (or the highest clef his instrument uses), starting on the thumb as line one (the lowest line in that clef). Whenever the child says the lines or spaces of the staff, he must always say them up from the thumb to the fifth finger and from the first line to the fifth line. (As a matter of fact, whenever you describe music notation always say the note letters from the lowest note up, never from the top down.)

Use the left hand to say the lines of the bass clef or the lowest clef his instrument uses. In this case, the fingers of the left hand will face the opposite direction, with the fingertips going east (right), and the wrist west (left).

Similarly, using the spaces between the fingers, say the spaces of the two clefs using the space between the thumb and second finger as space number one. If the instrument only uses one clef, learn the next clef higher or lower, anyway. Every musician should know the notes of at least two clefs without having to laboriously figure them out.

Here's why: Let's say a soprano hears a song sung by a baritone. The soprano decides to learn the song, but she has to transpose it from the baritone's range (low) to the soprano's (high). The baritone sings in the bass clef. The soprano sings in the treble clef. She must know both clefs in order to move the music from the low notes to the high notes.

The child should always say the lines and spaces of each clef the same way, every time. Little by little the sentence should be said faster and faster, until it is all in one breath.

The child should wiggle each finger to indicate which line he is identifying at the moment each is said. When the child says the spaces, he should put the second finger of the left hand between each of the fingers of the right hand to indicate the spaces between the lines.

The following example uses the treble and bass clefs, but if the child's instrument only uses one clef, choose the next higher or lower clef and have the child learn that one as well.

- The lines of the treble clef are E, G, B, D, F (using the right hand).
- The lines of the bass clef are G, B, D, F, A (using the left hand).
- The spaces of the treble clef are F, A, C, E (using the right hand).
- The spaces of the bass clef are A, C, E, G (using the left hand).

The student should do this exercise twice a day, five minutes in the morning and five minutes at night, making many repetitions of each line.

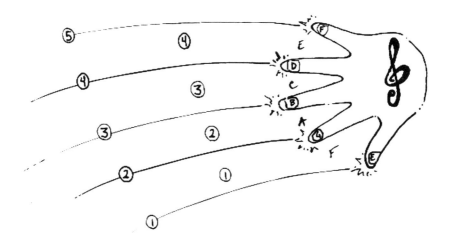

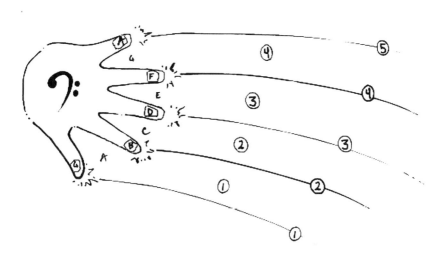

Note Recognition   Students learn to recognize the notes just by seeing them, the same way a child learns to recognize the word *c-a-t* as *cat* just by seeing the letters written together.

Direction of the Notes   Students should learn to watch the direction of the notes. If the notes go higher in the music, the hand should play higher sounds on the instrument. If the notes go down, the hand should play sounds that go lower. Although this method does not help a student to learn the notes themselves, the student will learn the direction in which to play.

Eyes Front, Heads Up Students should always look at the music, not at the hands. This, in combination with the other tips above, will accelerate the ability to read music. When we play by touch, mistakes help the fingers learn. It is actually better to allow the fingers to play the wrong notes. Then make corrections by listening to the sound and looking at the hands to see how far away they are from the valve, the string, or the correct note. I call that "learning *what* to do by learning what *not* to do."

Musicians learn to make big jumps from one note to another on their instrument without ever having to look at their hands or the instrument in much the same way as someone learns to hit the keys on a computer keyboard. Even if you only type on the computer with a couple of fingers, I am sure you have noticed that after a while your hands learn where the various keys are and the fingers go to them automatically without thinking and without having to look.

Learning to play by feel takes courage. You can't be wimpy about it. As much as possible, look at the music, and let your fingers find the notes. Of course, always look at the first note to get your bearings. After that, "let the fingers do the walking." Remember: eyes front, heads up!

FOR STUDENTS

Looking Back

Don't just pass over the *parents* section. The material there is as important for older students and adults as it is for parents and children. But you're not a parent, you say. Who cares? Look back up to what I have already written, and make use of anything you can from that section before going ahead. I think you'll find it very valuable.

Standing during Practice

Some students prefer to stand when they practice, at least part of the time. However, for students who can practice for comparatively long stretches of time, it's probably better to sit so that you don't become fatigued. In any case, standing even a short time doesn't work well for students who play larger instruments like the harp, the acoustic bass, the organ, the tuba, the trombone, and the piano. Come to think of it, after a while, standing to practice becomes tiring even if you're practicing a piccolo.

Sweeping Out the Cobwebs

As I said above, when you sit down to practice take a moment to relax and mentally focus. Shrug your shoulders, shake your head a few times (it's always good to shake out the cobwebs), and promise yourself to devote whatever time you have to concentrated practice. If you begin every practice with this ritual, it will soon become a habit, and you will find yourself able to shut out the outside world whenever you practice.

Organized, Focused Practice

Regardless of your age as a student, it is important that you practice as much as possible. Again, whether you practice in one fell swoop or spread it out is immaterial, and even if you don't practice as much as you would like, if the practice is consistently well-organized and purposeful, the results will be terrific.

Learning Music Notation

Again, everything in the section for parents under *music notation* needs careful study because it is as important for older students and adults as it is for children.

FOR INSTRUCTORS

Instructors who expect the best from their students usually find that the students give them 100 percent, sometimes even more. Those who ask for only 50 percent from their students may get even less. Therefore, it is always important that we be precise and knowledgeable in our explanations to students, responsive to any questions they have even if they don't know quite how to verbalize them, decisive in the training we give to them, and demanding of their respect, time, and effort without ever being degrading or demeaning.

Let your students know what you expect from them. Try to avoid phrases like, "It would be nice if you would . . ." If you want them to do something, let them know in no uncertain terms that this is what you want and that it will not be acceptable if they don't do it. Say things like, "This will be a challenge for you, and perhaps a little difficult in the beginning, but work at it, and it will improve. If you have any problems with it, feel free to call me. I'm always here to help."

Make lesson plans and roadmaps for students and parents, and be prepared to follow them, even when you are teaching students one-on-one. However, be sufficiently flexible to know when to hold back and when to press forward. Use the guidelines in the National Standards for Arts Education to insure that you set goals for your students and that your students can reach those goals.

Parents and students think that as the musical experts we know everything about music. The truth is, *we* know that we *don't*. I've often told my students that the more I learn about music the more I realize how little I know. Don't pretend to know the answers when you really don't, but make sure you let the parent or student who asks the question know that you will do the research and find out the answer.

Be creative in the kind of teaching that you do. Wherever possible, use the students' own strengths, interests, and even weaknesses to help them learn. If a student likes video games, find musical video games that will teach as well as entertain. If a student doesn't understand fractions, teach them to him through the mathematics of music. If a student has a bent for technology and would rather be at the computer than anywhere else, keep an eye out for computer programs that will enhance your teaching. Find ways to connect the student's real life and musical life. Remember that good music instruction teaches so much more than just music: The attention to detail that our students develop through practice helps them in everything else they do in life. The goal-setting skills they learn when they strive to make a music composition performance-ready help them when it's time to write a college term paper or spend months job seeking. The self-confidence a student builds through the small successes in learning music becomes very important when going out into the big world. What students learn in the music room doesn't stay in the music room; it affects the rest of their lives.

Don't become stagnant in the way that you teach. The good old days that you remember are gone. If you long for the days when teachers hit their students' hands with rulers to make them listen, find instead a way to strike their minds so that they will say to themselves, "Wow, that's a great idea!" And if you find yourself feeling a little left out because the world is changing too quickly, do some updating on yourself. Take some courses, and learn something that will help you to live better and work better in today's world. If we expect to help our students to be the best that *they* can be, then as instructors, we owe it to ourselves and them to be the best that *we* can be.

And, most of all, always remember to temper everything you teach, everything you say, and everything you do with understanding, a little love, and a whole lot of humor.

8

RISOLUTO

To Count or Not to Count? 'Tis Not a Question

Perhaps of all the most basic elements of music, rhythm most directly affects our central nervous system.

—George Crumb, composer

PRELUDE

Terry was quite upset. The music that he played for his teacher didn't sound anything like the CD of the music that was written on the page before him. He pointed at it with his violin bow. "I just can't play this right," he fumed. His face knotted up into a grimace. "No matter how many times I do it, it's always wrong. And it's annoying, really annoying, because I know the song. I know what it's supposed to sound like. And this just doesn't sound like the song. I think they wrote the wrong notes here or something," he complained. He hit the bow against the music stand, hard. The force of the blow made his white hair stand up on end.

"Did you count it when you practiced it?" asked his teacher, gently.

"No, I just tried to learn the notes first. That gives me a leg in the door, and then, after I know the notes I learn the rhythm. That's how I learn everything."

"That's the long way. I'll show you another way that helps you learn it faster. Let's play it and count it out loud. Come on. Do it slowly."

"Please, don't make me count. I hate it. It's embarrassing. It makes me feel like a little kid. And, besides, it's so much harder to play and count at the same time. I can't do everything at once. I get confused."

"But that's the easiest way to do it. Then you know where every beat is. Come on, let's try. We'll do it together. Here, let's just do a couple of measures. We'll do it very slowly."

Terry answered the instructor in an agitated tone, "Alright, I'll try it, but I really feel like I'm being treated like a child."

"Oh, I'm sorry," answered the teacher. "I didn't mean to sound like I was treating you like a child. How about this? Instead of playing and counting, let's just clap the music in time and count it so that you hear what the rhythm should sound like."

"Okay, I didn't mean to jump at you, but I am so irritated. I know what the whole song sounds like, but I just can't do it."

"Sure you can. Here, let's just clap the rhythm. We'll do it from here." The instructor pointed to the music. "We'll just do these four measures. Are you ready? I'll count four first, and then we'll start. One and two and three and four and . . ."

They counted the rhythm in the four measures. When they finished, the instructor said, "That was great. You clapped it exactly correctly. The rhythm was perfect."

Terry answered, "Hmm. Okay, I have to admit, that wasn't too tough. How about we do four more measures?"

"Great. Here we go. I'll count four beats first. One and two and three and four and . . ." They clapped the rhythm in the next four measures.

Terry chuckled. "That really wasn't hard. But I'm telling you, I can't both play and count at the same time."

"Sure you can. I'm gonna show you. Watch. We'll do just one measure, okay? Pick up your violin. Get your bow ready. Really slow now. Just the first measure. Here we go. I'm gonna count—one and two and three and four and . . ."

Terry played the measure. Notes, rhythm—it was all correct. He turned to the instructor and said, "Okay, but that was just one measure. I can't do the whole thing like that. It's too hard."

"Stop thinking 'No, I can't,' because you can. I want you to do one measure at a time, just like we did the first measure. Let's do measure two now. Come on. Are you ready? Really, really slowly now. Here's the count—one and two and three and four and . . ."

Terry played the second measure with the correct notes and rhythm. "Well, it looks like I owe you an apology. It really does seem easier like this.

But I have to do it one measure at a time," he said. He was smiling from ear to ear.

"That's how you should practice anything, in teeny measures, so that you can make sure the notes and the rhythm are correct. You can't have one without the other."

Terry chuckled. "I guess I have been practicing wrong. I'll go home and try again. Thanks for straightening me out. This has been a wonderful lesson, in more ways than one," he said.

"Good. By next week I bet you'll have learned the whole section—notes and rhythm—and it will sound like the CD you've been listening to. It will be slower, but you'll recognize that it is the same piece."

"Thank you. I really mean it. Thank you very much for today."

"You're welcome. Anytime."

FOR EVERYONE

Rhythm "makes the world go 'round," to paraphrase Fred Ebb's lyrics in the Broadway musical *Cabaret*. Everything has rhythm. Life has a rhythm. Poetry has rhythm. There is rhythm in the rotation of the Earth. There is even a rhythm to childbirth. And, of course, music has rhythm—lots and lots of rhythm.

We not only hear rhythm, we feel it. When the rhythm is "balanced," it feels good. When it isn't, it feels uncomfortable. A good horseback rider develops a rhythm that synchronizes his movement with that of the horse. When that happens, we say the rider is "at one" with the horse. The rider and the horse work together, beautifully balanced.

On the other hand, if the wheels of a car are not properly aligned and balanced, the car develops an up-and-down bouncing motion and a nasty *clunkety-clunk* sound.

Someone who enjoys amusement-park rides develops a body rhythm that matches the movement of the ride, and the ride feels exciting, yet comfortable. Me? Whenever I get on one of those rides my stomach knots up, I turn green, and I vomit; but that's another story.

What Is Rhythm?

What, then, *is* rhythm, and why is it so important? Rhythm is a variety of longer and shorter pulses in combination that creates a sense of motion in life and makes everything around us sound interesting, Without it, all we'd ever hear is a monotonous drone—a never-ending *dum-dum-dum-dum-dum* (and even that repeated many times becomes a kind of rhythm, albeit a boring one). Because the constant *dum-dum-dum-dum-dum* is so repetitive, little by little people would tire of the monotony of the sound, begin to ignore it, and, eventually, just stop hearing it altogether.

I live rather close to a railroad crossing where cargo trains pass on the street day and night. When we first moved into our home the sound of the moving trains used to drive me absolutely wild. The sound was deafening; it was irritating and interfered with everything I did. It even woke me several times during the night. In order to do any work during the day I had to consciously ignore the sound, and I had to put a pillow over my head to get to sleep at night. Now I am so used to the sound that not only does it not bother me, but I really don't even hear it anymore.

Rhythm Is Important in Music

Rhythm is so important that in some cases the listener can identify a song by its rhythm alone. If you clap the rhythm of "Happy Birthday," you can almost hear the tune in your head while you are clapping, can't you? Go ahead, try it:

> Hap-py birth-day to you-oo,
> Hap-py birth-day to you-oo,
> Hap-py birth-day, dear John-ny,
> Hap-py birth-day to you-oo.

There, you see? When you clap it in the correct rhythm, the unsung melody meshes with the claps so well that you can practically hear the melody in the background. That's how important rhythm is.

In many respects, rhythm is more important than melody. We can have rhythm without melody (think about rap music and hip hop) but not melody without rhythm.

There used to be an interesting, if fanciful, tale about how people could die if they were to listen to a drum played at a steady pace of sixty beats per minute for a long while that was then, little by little, slowed down until, eventually, the drum beats stopped altogether. The theory was that as the drum beat slowed down, so did the person's heart beat, and when the drum was finally silent, the heart would stop beating entirely. Frankly, I haven't tried it, and I wouldn't recommend it, but it is an interesting story, nevertheless.

Counting Helps Students Understand Rhythm

Because it is so vital to all of life and especially to musicians, understanding rhythm is a necessary part of all music learning. To understand the rhythm of a piece of music, students must be able to count it. And therein lies the rub! Students, regardless of age, hate to count, at least when they're playing music, because they think it will confuse them. Of course, they don't have any problems counting when it comes to money, time, or toys, but when it comes to music . . . uh-oh.

Shortcuts Don't Work

Students often think that they can learn the melody of a piece first and worry about the rhythm later. This wastes a lot of time and causes the student to take much longer to learn a piece of music. Remember that the object of this book is to optimize practice and minimize the time it takes to get results. With that in mind, think about this:

- A piece played in the wrong rhythm doesn't sound anything like the same piece played with the correct rhythm. To demonstrate this, I often play the melody of "The Star-Spangled Banner" for students with the correct melody but in the wrong rhythm, with long notes where they are supposed to be short and short notes where they should be long. When I ask students to identify the piece of music, they can't. When the rhythm is played incorrectly, the song just doesn't sound like anything they know.
- If you try to learn the notes of a piece without thinking about the rhythm, you will probably hold each note the same length of time. Although you think you are playing without rhythm, playing all the notes the same length of time *is* a rhythm. Unfortunately, it's the wrong rhythm. If you learn the piece with the wrong rhythm first, you'll have to relearn it in the right rhythm eventually if you ever want to play it correctly.
- If you try to fix the rhythm after you learn the notes, you'll already have the sound of the wrong rhythm in your head. Now you'll have to unlearn the wrong rhythm before you can substitute the right rhythm. Why take double the time to learn the piece when you could do it right in the first place?

Learn to Count

The solution is to learn to count and play at the same time. If you learn to count whenever you practice, you will develop what I call an *inner clock*. This inner clock will fast track you toward understanding the mathematics of music in any piece you play.

The best and most productive way to learn to count and play is to do the counting *out loud*, but that isn't possible for all instrumentalists. Keyboard players, guitarists, string players, harpists, and percussionists can count out loud and play at the same time, but woodwind and brass instrumentalists can't because they have only one mouth (unless there's somebody out there that I don't know about who has two mouths). Wind players learn to count by tapping the foot while they play, but that isn't really as effective as counting out loud. Unfortunately, they don't have a choice.

Another method is to write the numbers of the counts underneath each beat of music and then clap the music according to the counts that have been written. This method is not quite as effective as counting out loud, but it works and is most effective when it is used in conjunction *with* counting out loud. First the student writes the counts under the notes, then claps them, and then plays them according to the way they were clapped.

Some students try to use a *metronome* to count for them instead of counting themselves. Metronomes have a different purpose altogether. The click of the metronome helps the student keep the *tempo* of the piece steady (if the student plays exactly with it). It doesn't help the student play the different rhythmic values of the notes. All the metronome does is beat time. It is up to the player to know the value of each note and be able to play it rhythmically correctly.

Rhythmic Values

Before going any further, let's identify the basic kinds of notes we use in music. It's all quite mathematical; so if you understand it in math, you'll get it in music. If you don't, well, this is your chance to learn.

A whole note is the longest note we have. (Well, there actually *is* one longer note, but it is used so seldom that we won't bother with it here.) Think of a whole note as a whole pizza. It even looks like a pizza; it's a round, white circle. And, like a pizza, if you cut it in two halves, you get two half notes. When you cut two half notes in half, you get four quarter notes. When you cut four quarter notes in half, you get eight eighth notes, and so on, down the road, all the way to two-hundred-fifty-sixth notes. Simply stated, each note is assigned a time value, and the next note in line is twice as fast as the one before it. Therefore,

one whole note	= two half notes,
one half note	= two quarter notes,
one quarter note	= two eighth notes,
one eighth note	= two sixteenth notes,
one sixteenth note	= two thirty-second notes,

and so on. There. You see? It's not very complicated at all. Oh, I almost forgot: we use the words *count* and *beat* more or less interchangeably. So when we say that "this has four counts," we could also say that "this has four beats," and it would mean the same thing.

Every Beat Has Two Parts

When counting, it is important to remember that each beat really has two equal parts, the first half and the second half. To demonstrate this, think of tapping your hand on a table. The hand goes down and hits the table. That's the first part of the beat. In order to hit the table a second time, you must raise your hand again. That's the second half of the beat. Try it as you read this. Do it in rhythm.

Lower the hand and hit the table.
Raise the hand and start again.
Lower the hand and hit the table.
Raise the hand and start again.

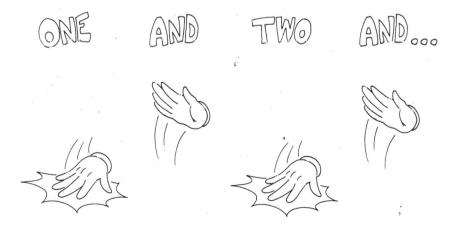

We call the first half of the beat a number (1, 2, 3, 4, and so on), and we call the second half of the beat *and*. Each beat has a number plus the *and*. When you write out the beats, clearly indicate both parts of each beat.

Likewise, always *count* both parts of every beat. If we are counting quarter notes, the first part of the quarter note (which is really an eighth note) gets the number, and second part of the beat (the eighth note) is its *and*. If we are counting eighth notes, the sixteenth note is the *and*. If we are counting sixteenth notes, the thirty-second is the *and*, and so on. If you know where the *and* part of the beat is, you can count anything.

FOR PARENTS

Children—especially young children—don't like to count during practice, and getting them to do it, externally, internally, or any other way, is a real challenge. They do, however, like rhythm and often engage in repetitive, rhythmic activities. Here are a couple of specific ideas for getting your child to think rhythmically about the piece he is playing:

Pounding Out the Rhythm

Have the child beat the rhythm of the part being played on a drum, a tambourine, or, even better, pots and pans. The idea of beating time on pots and pans may sound silly (and might be louder than you would like), but that's exactly what makes it so effective. It adds an element of fun to the learning process. The more a child enjoys doing something, the more he will do it. Have the child beat the time of only a few measures and repeat it five or six times until he understands the rhythm in his head. You could even have the child play the rhythm first on a drum, then on a tambourine, then on a pot or pan. This doesn't just create variety; it also causes the child to make more repetitions. And in practice the more repetitions we can get the child to make, the sooner he learns the rhythm. Then, finally, after the child has beaten the rhythm of a few measures on anything that will make a nice loud noise, ask him to play it on the instrument.

Renaming Notes for Little Children

For children who are too young to understand the relationships between whole notes, half notes, quarter notes, and eighth notes, identify the notes this way:

a whole note is called *ve-ry long note*,
a half note is *long note*,
a quarter note is *short*,
a dotted half note is *long note dot*,
an eighth note is *tee*, and
two eighth notes are *tee-nee*.

Reciting the Notes Out Loud

Since younger children (six and under) will be studying the piano, a stringed instrument, or a guitar, they *can* count the rhythm out loud. Therefore, the aim is to get them to *do* it. Naming the types of notes as they play them is easier than saying numbers and will insure that the rhythm is correct. Just make sure that they say them in such a way that

Two *long notes* takes the same time to say as one *ve-ry long note*

Ex: Ve-ry	Long Note
Long Note	Long Note

Two *shorts* take the same time to say as one *long note*

Ex: Long Note	Long Note
Short Short	Short Short

Two *tee-nees* takes the same time to say as one *short*

Ex: Short	Short	Short	Short
Tee-nee	Tee-nee	Tee-nee	Tee-nee

and so on. Counting by saying the kinds of notes being played is a wonderful exercise not just for youngsters but for older students and adults as well, because it clarifies the exact fractional relationships between the notes.

Rhythm Imitation

Another exercise that children enjoy teaches rhythm through imitation. First you choose a simple rhythm and clap it. Then the child must repeat the rhythm exactly as you do it. To insure success, don't make the rhythm too difficult, especially in the beginning. Make up another rhythm, and have the child clap it. Each time the child imitates the rhythm you clap correctly, make the next one a little more complex. If the child has trouble imitating the rhythm exactly, back off and make the next one easier. Alternate the instruments the child uses to imitate the rhythms. Use hand clapping, small drums, tambourines, even pencils beating on a table. And occasionally ask the child to create the rhythm that you will imitate.

FOR STUDENTS

Students often think of rhythm as being in the background and less important than the tune. Counting brings rhythm to the foreground and makes it easier to understand and easier to play correctly.

For those students who don't use their mouth when playing, it is very important to count out loud. Counting out loud is meant *to get your attention*. If it is annoying to you, remember that that is exactly its purpose. Counting out loud is supposed to make you consciously aware of where every beat and every half beat goes. For those who can't count out loud, tap your foot and count inside; but one way or another you must count when you play. Counting out loud is easier than counting to yourself, because, when done correctly, it sounds as if someone else is right there in front of your face pointing out the beats. You become immediately aware of a mistake if your mouth says "three and," yet you are playing the first beat in a measure. When that happens, a light flashes inside your head, and a voice says, "Whoops—what did I do?" It's a way of catching your mistake in the moment that it is made.

If you find that coordinating saying and playing is difficult for you, choose a very small amount of music, like one measure, play it very slowly, and force yourself to count it. In the first few minutes it will be a challenge, but it won't be long before you can do it accurately and easily. Then try another measure. When you are trying to learn how to count, always choose a small amount of music, play it very slowly, and count it very loudly. Eventually, you will be able to count the piece all the way through.

Regardless of whether you count out loud or to yourself, do it *all* the time, not *some* of the time or *most* of the time. Count every beat of the piece, from the moment you start playing to the moment you stop.

Sometimes students start out counting but, as they get further into the piece, they become so involved in reading notes and playing accurately and musically that they stop counting. It's very important to continue counting throughout the piece.

Don't start to count, then stop, and then start counting again later on in the piece when you suddenly remember that, "Oops, I haven't been counting." You must count continuously throughout the piece so that the beat stays constant. If you start to count after not doing it, you won't know what speed to count at and will, almost certainly, begin counting at a pace that is slower or faster than the speed at which you played.

Don't stop counting when you get to a part that is hard to play. It's even more important to count during the parts that are difficult. If a piece is too hard to count and play at the same time, first try clapping the notes and counting without playing the notes.

Even if you *can* count out loud, try writing in the numbers of the counts under the music, and don't forget to put in the *and* of every beat exactly under the note or notes to which it's assigned. Writing in the beats is a really good way of learning where every beat is.

When you count, look at the music and say the counts you wrote there. Keep it simple. Just speak whatever you wrote. There should be the number *1* under (or over) the note that is the beginning of the first beat in the measure and an *and* under or over the note that starts the second half of the beat. Similarly, there will be a *2* under the second beat note and its *and* under the second half of the beat, and so on. If the note that starts the beat contains both halves of the beat, then just write the number plus the *and* under that note.

Practice slowly, and make sure you understand every division of the beat. Keep counting. For those of you who can count out loud, make sure you do! Don't mumble the count. Counting works best when it is loud enough to keep the student aware of what he is saying. In other words, you have to hear what you're saying in order for it to bother you when you aren't playing the same beat that you are saying.

There really is no choice. If you want to play any kind of music accurately and comfortably, you must have an understanding of the rhythm of the

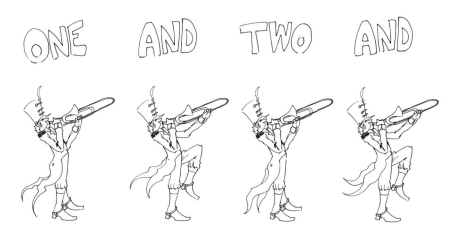

piece. You *must* count. Count inside, count outside, count upside down, but count. Like any other part of music, it requires a little training. However, mastering counting is much easier than it sounds, and it takes years off the learning process. I guarantee that if you count for two months straight, you will get so used to it that you'll feel lost when you don't. Come on, you can do it. I know you can. Give it a whirl. *One and two and three and four and . . .*

FOR INSTRUCTORS

One of the big challenges that music instructors face is teaching students to appreciate the importance of rhythm. Students—especially those students who don't like math in the first place—often have a difficult time recognizing the close connection between mathematics and musical time values. Sometimes it seems like the only ones interested in the mathematics of music are the percussionists. Percussion students live for rhythm. Give them a pencil, and they'll drum on a desk. Give them two pot covers, and they'll clang away happily all day. Give them an empty conch shell and something to hit it with, and they'll make music for a week. But the rest? Not so easy.

Regardless of how daunting it seems, we must impress on our students that without rhythm there is no music, and without being able to count we won't understand the rhythm.

Even though it takes time from the lesson, we must make the student grasp the concepts of the mathematics of music. We must explain again and again, and yet again, about the division of beats, how it happens, when it happens, and how it must be counted. Sometimes it takes weeks, sometimes it takes months, and sometimes it seems like it takes forever. Nevertheless, we must persevere. Ultimately the student will get it.

Don't try for any shortcuts. Insist that students count, regardless of age. Insist that they count the half part of the beat (the *and*) as well as the primary part of the beat, throughout the piece. Some students say, "one, two, three, four and," saying the *and* only where it happens to be in the music. If there isn't an *and* note after each beat, they don't say it. Tell them to be precise. If there is an *and* at the end of beat four, there is also an *and* after beats one, two, and three. They must hear the *and* after each beat that they say.

Some students don't understand that the *and* isn't always an eighth note—that whatever kind of note gets one beat, the next faster note value note is the *and*. Because elementary music so often uses the quarter note as the beat note, students get used to thinking of the eighth note as the *and* not realizing that if an eighth note is the beat, then a sixteenth note is its *and*, and that if we are counting each half note as one beat, then the quarter note is the *and*. It is important to drill this concept into the minds of students.

If a student plays an instrument that makes counting out loud possible, then make sure the student counts loud enough to hear his own voice loud and clear. Sometimes the student should count louder than the playing. Counting softly in an undertone soon becomes mumbling, and mumbling becomes silence after the first ten measures.

Again, there really is no choice. If we want our students to understand and make use of rhythmic concepts, then we must make sure they count every piece they play from beginning to end, until it becomes so much a part of them that the clock inside their musical soul begins to tick automatically.

⑨

TOCCATA

Learned Automatic Motion (LAM)

Practice without improvement is meaningless.

—Chuck Knott, American football coach

PRELUDE

Tim paced back and forth as he talked on the telephone to his instructor. He was very agitated. "So, how did the party go last week, Tim?" the instructor asked.

"The party went fine. My playing didn't. I've never been so embarrassed in my life. I was absolutely mortified."

"Why? What happened?"

"I was so sure I knew the piece by memory. I had practiced it so many times that I could've done it in my sleep. Then, when the moment came to play it, I blew it. The whole world was there—my wife, my mother and father, all my friends. The living room was filled with people. Everyone was sitting comfortably after a good meal, and someone asked me to play, so I sat down at the piano. If I had known what was going to happen, I would have run out the door and gone far, far away. How could I possibly have disgraced myself so badly? I just can't understand why it happened.

"I announced the piece I was going to do and started to play. At first, everything went smoothly. Even though I was a little nervous, inside I felt pretty good. There I was, playing my fingers off. Everything was going fine. All of a sudden, one of my wife's friends moved a little bit in her armchair. I didn't really even see her. I certainly wasn't looking at her. I just sort of heard the movement as I played, and I got distracted."

Tim began to speak faster. His voice became more agitated. "Suddenly, I forgot everything I was doing. I had no idea where I was in the piece or what the last few notes were that I had played, and I couldn't figure out a place in the piece that I could jump to. At home, I always played the piece from the beginning, so I didn't know another place from which I could start."

"Maybe that's what was wrong," his instructor said. "Do you remember what I said about finding several places to start from and practicing as if those places were the beginning of the piece so that if something happens during a performance, you have places you can start from without going back to the beginning?"

"Yes, I remember you said that, but I just never got around to finding those places and practicing them like that. I guess I should have."

His instructor continued, "So, tell me what happened."

"I couldn't even remember what the piece sounded like. Worse than that, I couldn't even remember the name of the piece, much less what page I was on or where I should go. I was totally and completely lost.

"Anyhow, in that one second, everything was suddenly gone from my head. It was as if I had never, ever played the stupid piece before. When I started to play, I was a little nervous, I'll admit, but it wasn't just about nerves. It was more like a demon took over, or a computer virus and destroyed everything I had worked toward for months. Delete, delete, delete. I was mortified. My brain was suddenly empty. Nothing. Zilch. I couldn't play one note. You can't believe the way I felt. I was so embarrassed. I wouldn't want to go through that again for anything in the world.

"I just don't understand why it happened. I practiced it until I was blue in the face. My fingers knew every turn, every cross over, every thumb under. Then, all of a sudden, just because one person moved and I wasn't expecting it, the fingers couldn't remember what to do. That's it. I'm done. I'll never play for anyone again. I don't even want to play for myself again. Why would anyone go through that humiliation by choice?"

The teacher answered, "Sometimes that happens when students don't know what to do to prevent it. Listen—you're coming for a lesson tomorrow, aren't you?"

"I'm not sure. To tell you the truth, I was thinking about stopping lessons altogether. I am so frustrated and annoyed at myself, and I just don't see how I can make this right."

"That's what teachers are for. Together we'll make it right. Just come, and I'll show you ways to avoid having this ever happen again. Perhaps the first time we talked about this you didn't understand how important the way you practice is. The secret is all in the practice."

"Perhaps you're right. Maybe I didn't understand, or maybe I just didn't think it was important. Okay. I'll come tomorrow."

"Don't worry. I promise to teach you how to fix this, and after you understand what to do, what happened at the party will never happen again."

"Okay. See you tomorrow."

FOR EVERYONE

There are many elements musicians must master in order to play a piece of music with any degree of proficiency. We must be able to

- read the music and understand how the composer wants it to sound,
- count so that the mathematics of the music is correct,
- keep the *tempo* (speed) uniform throughout the piece unless otherwise noted,
- execute the notes correctly in the proper speed (I don't mean kill the notes but, rather, to be able to play them) without thinking about them,
- emphasize the notes that require emphasis,
- get gradually louder or softer,
- play so that the notes are as smooth as silk, or as sharply separated as little drops of rain, and, finally,
- be able to forget all of the above (because by that time we hope they will be automatic) and just think about those things that enable us to make beautiful music.

You're probably thinking, "But I just want this for a hobby. Why do I have to learn all that? I just want to be able to play a few songs and make them sound pretty. I don't want to be a concert player." Maybe not, but even if we only play for our own enjoyment and no one else ever hears us, we must be in control of what we play. If we have that control, the music sounds and feels better in the hands, and we play it without stress.

LAM Is Control without Thinking

To achieve that control, one of the first things musicians must acquire is what I call *Learned Automatic Motion* (LAM). LAM is a set of movements that the body muscles, nerves, and brain learn to do automatically after many repetitions. Eventually these motions become a habit.

Let's say a golfer practices hitting an itty-bitty ball for months until he can control where it goes, how far it goes, and how fast it goes. After hundreds, maybe thousands, of repetitions, when he hits the ball nineteen times out of twenty it travels 250 yards through the air to a little hole in the ground. That's Learned Automatic Motion. (And grown-ups do this for fun and profit?)

LAM Is the Mechanics of Playing Automatically

Through LAM we teach the fingers:

- the distances between notes on a fingerboard,
- how far away each valve is,
- how high one must lift a finger to find a black key after playing a white key, and
- how to get from one place on an instrument to another quickly without looking.

Using LAM, musicians' hands feel and remember:

- how hard to press a string down,
- how much pressure is needed to draw a bow,
- how and where to press a valve to play the right note,
- how much breath is needed to blow a particular note on a wind instrument,
- when to hold a note down,
- when to release it,
- how to play the note loud or soft,
- how to play a note short or long, and
- how to play it fast or slow, all automatically.

Musicians call this *technique*. It sounds like a tall order, doesn't it? That's exactly why it takes so much practice.

After the body learns the automatic movements, there are many other things that are *not* automatic that we must do in order to play music well. It's not enough to know *how* to play a note soft and to be able to do it automatically. We must know *when* to play it soft in order to make it sound beautiful. It's not enough to know *how* to make the notes get gradually louder automatically in an exciting part of the music. The student must know *when* to do it, and exactly *how much*, and be able to do it so that it brings the audience to the edge of the seat. That takes musicianship, not technique, and that's another subject altogether.

It's sort of like watching a gymnast on the balance beam. It's technique when a gymnast can make those somersaults and pirouettes with perfect balance every time on four inches of wood without falling off, but it takes much more than technique to make the audience want to get up there and learn how to do it because it looks sooo easy. Incidentally, the gymnast must learn to make all those moves accurately on the balance beam in the same way musicians learn to play the notes accurately, except that gymnasts fall off the beam while learning it, whereas music students hopefully don't fall off the chair. (Perhaps that's why Victor Borge, the great Danish comedian, strapped himself to the piano bench with a seat belt during one of his Las Vegas routines.)

Musicians have to coordinate many elements and do them all at the same time to make music happen. LAM allows us to put some of the elements on automatic pilot so that we can concentrate on those elements requiring conscious thought when we play musically.

LAM is a kind of finger or hand memory. Finger memory is very different from the memory we use to learn a poem, spelling words, or telephone numbers by heart. That's *another* kind of memory that musicians have to learn.

After the musician can play by LAM, he still has to memorize in other ways to make sure that what is learned stays learned and doesn't become unlearned just because we are distracted.

Incidentally, have you ever wondered why people say they learn *by heart* when they mean *by memory*? Why don't they ever say *by feet* or *by stomach*? Oh yes, I forgot—doctors tell their patients to take pills *by mouth*. (What did they think we'd do with them, stick them in our eyeballs?)

LAM Requires Repetition

In order to achieve this finger memory we must repeat each move exactly the same way many, many times until the fingers learn it and remember it. If we don't repeat it enough, the hands won't be able to execute the move consistently. (There's that word *execute* again.) If we learn the passage using the wrong technique, the hands will learn it incorrectly, and then we will have to fix it. Patience, time, and lots and lots of repetition are needed to learn to play a piece of music accurately without consciously thinking about it. Without a doubt, learning it correctly right from the start is the quickest way to achieve that goal.

FOR PARENTS

Children, as well as adults, need to be able to play by Learned Automatic Motion. There are so many elements that we must put together when playing a musical instrument, or doing *anything* that requires coordination, that *some* of those elements must be automatic.

It is often very difficult to get young children to make enough repetitions of a musical composition so that their hands and fingers play it automatically. Parents must sometimes find creative ways to encourage the child to do what the child *must* do without allowing him to slip into doing what he *must not* do. Read, study, and use the material in the *For Students* section for ideas. Keep in mind that the more you vary the way the child makes repetitions, so long as the child maintains the same movements and position of the parts of the body that are required to *make* the movement, the sooner the child will learn to make the movement automatically.

One Case History

Samantha, a young intermediate piano student, came to her lesson very frustrated because she couldn't learn a certain part of a piece. She told me that she had worked on it very hard for several days. Almost in tears, she said, "I think I have to stop music lessons. This is too hard. I can't do it. I must be stupid or something. I tried and I tried and I tried."

I said, "First of all, never say 'I can't do it.' Say 'I can't do it, *yet.*'"

"Okay," she yelled, "I can't do it, *yet*. I really tried. I feel so stupid." She reached up to the music stand and punched the music. It fell to the floor with a thud.

Quietly, I explained, "Second of all, *you* can do it. It's the *fingers* that can't, yet. I bet you know exactly what to do when you get to that part. Your fingers just can't do what you tell them. It's not you; it's the *fingers.*"

"My fingers are a part of me. It's the same thing," she answered, wiping the tears from her face with the back of her hand. She kicked at the music on the floor.

"No, it's not," I said. "As a matter of fact, that's exactly the point. You must learn to think of your ten fingers as if they were ten children, ten naughty children, who won't do what you tell them. Can you do that?"

"How will that help?" she asked. She had stopped crying and was beginning to listen.

"If you can think of your fingers as separate people from you, you'll be able to guide them better," I said. "They need to work more at the parts they can't do. If you keep them at it, eventually they'll learn what you want them to learn. Don't let them get away with anything. Be firm with them. Think of them as your children. Would you let your children do anything they wanted?"

"Of course not," Samantha answered. "Are you saying that if I tell them what to do they'll obey me?" By this time, she was hanging on to every word I said.

"Not right away, but eventually they will. Because, just like a good parent, you'll be strict with them. After a while, they'll do what you say."

A little smile overtook her mouth. She giggled. Suddenly, she looked at me conspiratorially and asked me, "Can we name my fingers?"

"Sure," I answered. "But first, please pick up the music from the floor." She did, and then we named every one of her fingers.

Before she left the lesson, she said, "I'm going home, and I'm going to make them do it. I won't give them supper until they learn it. I won't let them watch television until they get it right. You watch. By next week, they'll learn it, or else."

When Samantha came for the next lesson, she was very pleased with herself. That is to say, she was very pleased with her fingers. She told me, "Sally" (her fourth finger) "tried to give me an argument, but after a while she stopped fighting with me and did it right."

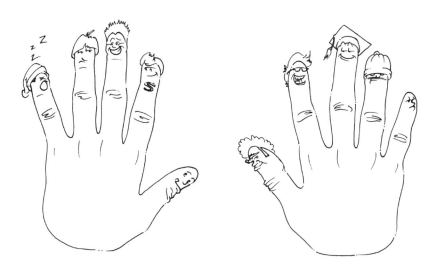

The lesson went beautifully. Samantha played the music without one mistake. It was absolutely great. "You see?" I said. "All it took was more work. Remember, you're the mom. You have to tell the fingers what to do and how to do it. Then you must see to it that they do it correctly, every time. Remember, for them to learn anything without having to think about it, they have to do it a lot. If your fingers can't do something *yet* it's because they just haven't done it *enough*. Be patient with them. You'll see, eventually, that they'll learn anything you want to teach them."

FOR STUDENTS

Students develop LAM eventually, whether they want to or not. Ultimately, when they have made enough repetitions for the fingers, hands, and arms to remember a movement of any kind, that movement becomes automatic and the student does it without conscious thinking. At that point, whether the student does the movement correctly or incorrectly depends entirely on how he practiced it and how much thought went into that practice. Anything we learn wrong we must eventually relearn until we get it right. Therefore, making the muscles and nerves react correctly from the very beginning is a great way to shorten practice time and to insure a correct result. Here are some ideas for developing LAM correctly, right from the start:

Practice Really Small Sections

Tackle short segments of the piece at a time. What you, as a student, may think is a small section may, in fact, be much too much for your hands to learn. The music may look simple, but it isn't, and though you may think a half page of elementary music isn't very much (usually about eight or twelve measures), to a *beginning student* it's like learning a thirty-page speech. In Japanese.

It's much too hard for the brain and the hand to learn what to do if you work on too much at one time. Therefore, don't work on more than one or two measures at a time. If the section is complicated, do even less than that. There are many things to think about, and in order to play you must remember what they are and do them all at the same time. Here's a short list of what it takes to play even a beginning piece. You must remember:

- how to sit,
- the correct hand position,
- how to hold your fingers,
- what the notes are,
- where the notes are on the instrument,
- how to count so that the rhythm of the piece is correct, and
- how to play the notes in such a way that everyone hears them and not lose any notes along the way.

For a beginning student, that's a lot to think about. Practicing too long a section makes it take much longer to learn. By the time you get to the end of the part, because it goes on so long you'll forget to play solidly, or to count, or what the note is, or how to get there, or what finger to use, and so on, and you'll have to keep going back and doing it again and again, and you'll keep forgetting and forgetting, and it will take forever to learn. Have compassion on your fingers. The smaller the section you practice, the easier it will be to learn, and the sooner you'll learn it. Would you try to memorize a speech in Japanese all the way through if you were just learning Japanese? Of course not. The same principle goes for any instrument you play.

Again, and Again, and Again

Make many repetitions of very small parts. Many, many, many, many repetitions. What do I mean by *many*? You can play a teeny part ten, twenty, thirty times in less than five minutes. It's easy. The more times you repeat it, the sooner the hands learn it. If you are only playing a few notes and keep doing them over and over (with a brief pause in between each time), the hands learn them quickly.

Increase the Speed Gradually

Increase the speed a teeny bit each time you make a repetition absolutely correctly. Oh, and don't get faster *during the repetition*. If you keep increasing the speed each time you repeat the passage correctly, you will ultimately arrive at the speed at which it is supposed to be played.

Use a Metronome

Try using a metronome to help you increase the speed of the passage very gradually. (You know what a metronome is, don't you? It's that wooden

tick-tock thing that used to sit on your grandmother's piano, only today it is no bigger than a credit card, is sleek-looking, has no pendulum, and, of course, is electronic.) It's a wonderful gadget. Using a metronome makes it possible to increase the speed in such minute increments that it's almost undetectable to the ear.

Adding Elements

Every time you add an element (something new to the part you are practicing)—more notes, another articulation, a new dynamic, another measure—start at a slower speed with the metronome, because now there is more to think about, and that makes the part harder. Then, again, gradually increase the speed.

This is particularly important: If you make a mistake while playing the repetitions, reduce the speed until you find a tempo at which you can do the part perfectly. Then repeat it at that speed at least three times. After that, begin increasing the speed once more.

Always Make Repetitions the Same Way

Once you know the notes and the rhythm, always practice with the exact same fingering and identical stretches and contractions of the hand. If you keep changing the way you do it, it will take longer for the fingers, hands, or mouth to learn the part.

Think about this: Let's say that you have moved to a new neighborhood and want to go to the supermarket. You ask directions, and someone tells you how to get there. He even writes the directions out for you. By following the directions, you get there—no problem.

A few days later, you have to go to the same supermarket, only you've lost the directions. Again, you ask someone. That person tells you a different way to go. You finally arrive at the store, but getting there feels like it's a whole new place, because nothing is familiar on the way.

The third time you go, you ask another person who gives you yet another set of directions. Although it's longer and again all the roads are new, eventually you get to your destination.

The fourth time you go . . . Well, you get the idea. Think how much sooner you would have learned how to get there if you had gone exactly the same way every time. Or maybe you should just send someone else to the supermarket.

How Large a Section to Practice

There are several ways to figure out how large a section to practice:

- If you are starting a new piece, try this: Being careful to count, and making sure the fingering is correct, play a passage of the music, and, at the first mistake, stop! And I mean the *teeniest stumble*. That's how far you should practice. Play it again and again and yet again to get it as even and as smooth as you can. Remember to make many repetitions and use the same fingering, motions, breath support, and/or lip pressure every time you play it.
- Another way to practice is to play from the beginning of the measure *before* a mistake to the first beat of the measure *after* the mistake. Make many repetitions. Do it until it's easy. Do it until it's *beyond* easy. Do it until your eyeballs fall out. My mother, who was a professional cymbalom player and a charter member of the musician's union in New York City, used to tell me, "If I wake you up at two o'clock in the morning and ask you to play the piece, if you really know it, you'll play it as well as if you did it at two o'clock in the afternoon." My mother was a wonderful person and a terrific musician. She had some problems with telling time, though. Anyhow, after you have fixed one mistake, start from *one measure before the end of the section you just worked on*, and continue *until the next time you make a mistake*. (Don't worry, it won't be long.) As soon as you mess up, stop. That's the next section to practice.
- If you know there are mistakes but you don't know *where* they are, play through the piece and make a mark in the music wherever there is a mistake. Then practice from the first beat of the measure *before* each mistake to the first beat of the measure *after* each mistake.
- Remember to practice the measures that connect the parts you are working on. If you practice measures one and two, and then measures three and four, be sure to practice measures two and three as well, in order to join both parts. Otherwise, you'll hesitate or stop between measures two and three. We call that "overlapping practice." You'll ultimately have to learn all the connecting measures to assure a smooth performance. Might as well do it at the beginning and save learning time.

Avoiding Boredom

The secret to avoiding boredom is to vary what you do with the notes. Play them quietly, play them loudly. Play them smoothly, play them jumpily. Play them in different octaves, but always remember to play them with the same technique, so that the muscles learn the motions.

How the Professionals Practice

Professional musicians have a whole bag of tricks for practicing a section without going crazy. I'll tell you a few of them, but don't you try it. These ideas are for *much* later when you are more advanced.

We invent creative rhythms with which to play the section. We play it with the wrong hand, or with unusual touches, or maybe even backward. (I've tried turning the music upside down to practice it that way, but it didn't work too well.)

More to Come

In the next chapters, you'll find a lot more ways to achieve the most benefit from practicing in the least possible time. There might even come a time when you don't have to practice at all. Now *that's* a thought.

By the way, if anyone ever invents a pill that teaches how to play music without practice, let me know right away. I'll be first in line to buy it. Oh, did you perhaps think that *I like practice*? Never! Not at all. Not even a *little* bit.

I hate practice just as much as everyone else . . . possibly even more. There is no doubt about it. Didn't you read the title of this book? *Practicing Sucks!* But it's necessary, and if you use at least some of these ideas to help you practice more productively, you'll discover, as I have, that the results are worth every second of work you put in.

FOR INSTRUCTORS

Instructors who teach students one-on-one have an advantage over classroom teachers in that we can concentrate on and individualize our instruction to meet the needs of a particular student much more readily than can those teachers who must work with many students at a time. It is important that we make use of that advantage by being as creative as possible in order to excite and inspire our students. It is not always necessary to be able to call all of the high-tech equipment available into play in order to be a good teacher (although being able to use *some* of it is a definite plus). Sometimes all that is necessary is being able to think outside the box a little bit.

As instructors we must learn to anticipate and hopefully manage situations that could potentially become problems for the student. It is important to tell students not just *what* to do but *how* and especially *why* to do it. It's not enough to tell a student to go home and practice a particular part in a piece in a particular way. Students need to know what to expect, what might happen, and what to do *if* or *when* it happens so that they will be in a better position to manage and control the inevitable frustration that occurs along the way.

It is important that the student play as much as possible during the lesson time so that the instructor can make whatever corrections are needed to help the student improve the pieces on which he is working. However, we must balance that with sufficient explanations (even when it takes away from the playing time) to enable the student to understand the reason the instruction is important. If the student doesn't know the reason for following a particular instruction, there's a good chance he just won't follow through.

Here's an example: Instructors often tell their elementary students to go home and practice a piece in small sections. However, they don't tell them what is *meant* by a small section or why it is so important. The student goes home, sees that the piece has only sixteen measures, decides to practice eight measures at a time (thinking that only eight measures *is* a small section) and then wonders why he can't learn it. *We* know why, though. The part the student is learning is just too long. Sadly, the student doesn't have the slightest clue that *that* is the problem, because the teacher didn't explain it.

Here's another example: An instructor tells a student to practice with a metronome, but the instructor doesn't explain the metronome's function or its limitations. Perhaps the student doesn't like to count and, without consulting the instructor, decides that the metronome can be used *instead* of the student's counting himself, since it "keeps time" like a clock. What the student doesn't know is that, although the metronome gives a regulated pulse, it doesn't help the student create time values and therefore is not a substitute for counting. The instructor should have explained that.

Here's another example using the same student and the same metronome. If the instructor doesn't teach the student how to practice with the metronome so that the beat of the playing meshes exactly with the click of the metronome, practicing with the metronome will be a total waste of time and will simply annoy the student. Ten minutes taken from the lesson to teach the student what he will hear if the music is played exactly with the metronome and what will be heard if he doesn't would fix this problem before it even emerges.

Teachers should give instructions in a manner that insures that the students understand what they want and why. If they don't understand after one explanation, we must try to find another way to explain it. We must use any means possible, no matter how silly, irrelevant, or outlandish it might seem, to make certain our students fully understand what we are teaching and can make use of the information in their practice and in their reactions to practice.

It's very important to not leave things to chance. It is better that the instructor be creative in the teaching rather than leaving the beginning student to become alarmingly creative during practice. If, instead of taking the time to make the necessary explanations, we leave things to chance, then there's an awfully good chance that the student will ignore or deviate from the instruction. Remember that if the students don't understand what we are telling them to do and why, if they don't get it, then they can't use it. And if they can't use it, then all our teaching efforts are in vain.

10

RITORNO VINCITOR

Victory over the Memory Monster

Everything learned by memory enriches us.

—Nadia Boulanger, teacher, composer, pianist

PRELUDE

The concert hall was filled to capacity with friends and family. One after the other, each student on the program had come dutifully to the stage to do their thing. It was 2:45 P.M. Greta was in the middle of her piece and doing just fine when . . . she realized that she was coming to a part that she had worked on a lot. Weeks, and weeks, and weeks just to get that one part. She thought to herself, "Oh, I hope I don't screw it up. It's just on the next page. Oh, I'm so worried—maybe I didn't learn it well enough . . ."

Suddenly, and for no reason at all, Greta's knees began to tremble. She couldn't stop them. From her thighs to her toes, everything was shaking. The floor under her feet felt like it was rocking back and forth and could collapse at any moment. "I bet everyone can see me shaking. I'll just sneak a peek." As her hands continued to play, she turned her head slightly to look out into the audience. In the shadows, she couldn't distinguish faces.

"Oh, boy, it's so dark out there, I can't see anything, and the light up here is so bright. It's really annoying. I never play with lights this bright. Why don't they turn the lights down a little so they don't glare in my eyes? Look at how the lights glitter against the instrument. Looks like starbursts. Makes it hard to see where to play."

In addition to her legs trembling, her heart began to pound, unevenly. She could feel it in her chest. She could actually hear it.

> Thump, thump
> Thump, thump
> Thump, thump
> Thump—

"Where's the second thump," she thought to herself. "I just want to get through this thing. My hands are so cold. Oh boy, I'm so dizzy. I'm going to pass out. Maybe I'm having a heart attack. Maybe I'm going to die right here on the stage."

Greta's fingers continued to move, but she could no longer hear the sound of the notes. She didn't know where she was in the music. And then, someone coughed in the audience. "Ohmigosh, what was that? A gunshot? Someone fell out there and broke a leg? A part of the wall fell down? An earthquake?"

It was 2:46 p.m. Greta's hands played a wrong note, or maybe a wrong finger, who knows? Suddenly, she was stuck. She couldn't go ahead. In midmeasure, she stopped playing. She simply stopped playing. "Oh boy, where am I? What's the next note? I don't remember what I just played. I know I wasn't at the part that I had trouble with. I don't know what comes next."

Tentatively, she tried out a few notes, hoping to find her place in the music. But she no longer remembered what piece she had been playing. Oh, she remembered the name of the piece, but she forgot how the music went. "Okay, I'll start from the beginning," she said to herself. And she lifted her hands to begin again. But the hands didn't remember how the piece started, not even the first measure, not even the first note. She couldn't even remember what key the piece was in or where to put her hands. She had absolutely no idea how to begin.

It was 2:47 p.m. With tears streaming down her face, she turned to the audience and sobbed, "I'm sorry, I can't do this. I just can't do this. I can't do this ever, ever again," and she ran off the stage, as if all the demons of hell were after her. Her teacher never saw her again. It took her twenty years to come back to music.

FOR EVERYONE

Musicians Develop a Repertoire

When professional musicians learn music, it stays in their fingers for many years and, in some cases, many decades. At the very least, professional musicians have hours and hours (maybe even days) of memorized music readily available for performance. They don't have to keep relearning pieces they have learned before in order to be able to play them. Over the years, one piece at a time, they build up a *repertoire*, a collection of hundreds of pieces of music of varying lengths, from three minutes to forty-five minutes, that they can play at will or on demand, all by memory. Sometimes they may have to play something they haven't even looked at in fifteen, twenty, twenty-five years, and, guess what? They can still play it. It may require a little polishing. They may need to fine tune it. But, basically, they can still play it even after a very long time. In order to do this, musicians must develop and maintain very good memorization skills.

Four Kinds of Memory

When musicians memorize, they don't just use one system to learn something. Their memorization skills incorporate four different senses and techniques: touch, kinesthesia, hearing, and sight. Learned Automatic Motion (LAM) is just one of them. (Taste isn't necessary, except in those cases where the student plans to eat the music, and neither is smell, unless the dog did something nasty on the pages.)

In order to memorize efficiently and to keep the material in the brain over a long time, musicians need to have the following:

- an aural memory of the sound of the piece being played;
- an analytical memory of everything that is written in the music including repeated patterns, key signatures, measures that are the same, and measures that have certain changes in them, the form of the piece, and so on;
- a visual memory that allows them to "read" the music even when it isn't there, remembering a coffee stain, the page number, how many lines there are, and where on the page the measure that we are currently playing exists (a kind of inner visual picture that we keep in our mind; the more detailed we can make that picture, the more it becomes useful as part of the memory process); and

- a kinesthetic memory that allows our nerves, our muscles, and our brain to remember and be able to physically reproduce every thumb turn, every finger crossing, and every contraction and expansion of the hand without thinking.

LAM Is Not Enough

Of all of the forms of memory, LAM is the easiest to learn. However, it takes the longest to learn, and, when used alone, it is often the least reliable. This is because in a sense it bypasses the brain altogether. Since the brain controls everything we do, nothing ever *really* bypasses the brain, but LAM bypasses *conscious* awareness. That means the fingers know where to go and can go there automatically even if the student isn't consciously aware of what the fingers are doing and sometimes doesn't even know where she is in the music.

LAM Is Like Sleepwalking

LAM is almost like sleepwalking. Have you ever gone for a walk and all the time you were walking you were thinking about something else? Suddenly you found yourself somewhere and didn't have any idea of how you got there or how long you had been walking. Using only LAM to play a piece of music is very similar. If some small distraction occurs, even the tiniest movement or sound, the fingers might get confused, and the student will lose her place and stop playing. Since the student wasn't too aware of where she was anyhow, it's difficult to pick up where she left off. LAM, used alone, is a very iffy kind of memorization. Too much is left to chance. Therefore, the best solution is to use a combination of all the different kinds of memory by getting the brain to work both consciously and subconsciously.

If We Didn't Memorize

Think about this: if musicians didn't memorize the pieces they play, they'd have to carry their music around with them in a suitcase—a very large suitcase—whenever there was a chance that they might be called on to play somewhere. What a scenario that would be. I can see it now:

Bob is spending the evening with friends. Someone asks, "Bob, how about you play something for us?"

"Of course," says Bob. "What would you like to hear—Chopin, Liszt, Schumann, Gershwin, Burt Bacharach, or John Lennon?"

"Schumann would be nice, and maybe a little John Lennon."

"Okay, I'll just go down the street to my car. It's in the parking lot. If I can see in the dark, I'll look through my music suitcase and find some Schumann and John Lennon. I'll be back before long. Um, anyone have a flashlight?"

"Don't you have anything you can play by memory?"

"No, I never memorize anything."

Hmm. Oops. Not a good answer.

Everyone Can Memorize Consciously

Many people believe they can't memorize. That's just not so. The truth is that everyone can learn to memorize consciously and in an efficient manner. It's not hard, but, like anything else, developing optimal memory skills requires knowing *what* to do, what *not* to do, and *how* to practice. The more often students memorize, the better they get at it. Remember, to make the best use of memory skills the playing can't just be automatic. The student has to be aware of absolutely everything she is doing at all times.

What's Wrong with Automatic Playing?

Those students who memorize by just blindly repeating something over and over and over until their fingers learn to play it automatically without thought, analysis, or knowledge do themselves a tremendous disservice. That kind of memory practically guarantees that the student will forget the piece within weeks of having memorized it, because she is leaving all the work to the fingers and none to the conscious awareness of the brain. As a result, that student really doesn't know the piece.

Automatic playing should be the last kind of memory work done, not the first. First, students should learn all the intricacies of the piece consciously, so that she is aware of every nuance, every pattern, every key change, every similarity and difference, every pedal move. In order to keep the piece in one's head for years and years, it should be completely analyzed from every angle and every possible viewpoint. Finally, after every other avenue of learning has been explored, exposed, and exhausted, then, and *only* then, should the student commit the piece to automatic playing.

Benefits of Learning Consciously

For elementary students there are many benefits to memorizing a piece efficiently and consciously instead of just by blind repetition: First of all, it gives us a tremendous advantage in the case of a memory lapse or some kind of mistake, in that it allows us to restart from practically anywhere in the piece. Learning only through automatic playing often means that if there is a glitch, the student will need to go back to the beginning of the piece and start again.

Learning to memorize consciously and efficiently increases and enhances brain productivity in younger people, and it helps to slow down brain-cell deterioration in the elderly. It is said that what is learned before the age of twenty-five either is retained or can be retrieved forever. Although it is easier for young people to memorize, older folks can do it also—it is just a little harder and takes a little longer. So what?

Memorizing consciously develops general intelligence, which is beneficial in many situations, not just where music is concerned. And, of course, memorizing consciously allows us to have a better understanding of what we learn.

These memorization skills work for everything. The best way to memorize anything is to make some kind of association to help you remember it—"ticklers" that you can use to help you connect to the words or meaning. These could be anagrams, formulae, patterns, word associations, numbers, or anything else you can think of. You do this all the time in other aspects of life. Why not apply the same thing to music?

FOR PARENTS

Young children don't generally use analytical techniques to learn. Rather, they learn by doing. As a result, their first and most natural way to memorize music is by automatic playing. Teachers so often hear the complaint, "Sarah works so long to learn a piece of music. She finally finishes it after months of work and two weeks after having learned it, she can no longer play it because she has forgotten it."

Even reviewing the pieces that have already been learned doesn't solve the problem, because eventually the child has too many pieces to review, and practice time gets used up reviewing instead of practicing. If the child only reviews what she has learned once a week or so, little by little the learning begins to deteriorate, the review becomes more and more shoddy, and ultimately the child forgets the piece anyway.

In order to help young children learn music in such a way that they remember what they have learned, parents must help them develop more sophisticated ways to memorize. Here are a few ideas that work particularly well for children. For details about these tips, please look in the *For Students* section:

- saying the notes: if the student learns to say the notes of the piece she is playing measure by measure, she will retain it longer;
- making associations in the music, places where the notes or rhythm are the same or similar, and places where there are chords or arpeggios or other kinds of notes worthy of being remembered;
- having the child memorize by choosing five or six places where she can start instead of only learning from the beginning of the piece;
- pointing out the page numbers (or some other mark in the music) where particular passages are and making the child think about visual associations (e.g., "Oh, there's a big crease in the music right here");
- having the child sing the notes without playing them; and
- having the child try to write the music out.

There are many other tips in the *For Students* section. Try out some of them, and see which work for your child. Remember that the most important thing the student must learn is that automatic playing is insufficient for retaining something that has been learned. In order to keep it in the memory banks, we have to be able to *understand* it and to be able to *make use* of it. Regardless of age, what we don't understand we can't use.

Think about how your child learns vocabulary words. She learns the word, how to spell it, how to write it, and how to put it into a sentence. It's exactly the same idea in music.

FOR STUDENTS

Following are some specific tips for developing conscious learning.

Separate the Hands

In addition to practicing with both hands together, spend a lot of time practicing hands separately. Ideally, you should be able to play through a whole piece, or at least a large portion of a piece, one hand at a time. This may sound like I am talking about mostly piano. That's not the case. The same idea goes for harp, organ, mallet instruments—any instrument that uses two hands. It even works with stringed instruments. You can practice only the left hand on the fingerboard and leave the bow on the music stand. For guitar you can practice first on the fingerboard and then work on the plucking. (And, please, I don't want to hear anything about a chicken.) For students of wind instruments, be creative: practice fingering the notes, but don't blow; or blow, but don't finger the notes.

Separate the Elements

Separating the elements for practice allows you to play faster than you could using all the elements, which is a good way to develop conscious memory skills and technique as well. When you add elements, add them only one at a time. Think about accuracy, or direction of the notes, or same/different, or technique, or musicality, but don't try to work with all the elements at once.

Change Speed, Volume

Consciously play every note very loudly or extremely softly. Practice slowly. Try to consciously think of everything that's in the music—accents, articulations, dynamics, direction of the notes, the kinds of notes, the speed at which they should be played, what happens before, and what happens after. Practicing slowly requires that you be continually aware of every aspect of the music.

On the other hand, another good way to memorize is to play fast automatically and force your mind to think of other things while you are playing. Try to pretend you are on stage and coping with the stage fright that you would be battling if you were actually in concert. Then pull your mind back to you, and make sure you can keep playing without missing notes.

Have someone sit in the room and cough or move in and out of the room, making sudden noises and unexpected disturbances, to see how well you can control your reactions in various situations.

Learn to Say the Notes

Choose a few measures of the music, and learn to say the notes by memory, away from the instrument. If the instrument that you are studying uses two staves, say the notes of only one staff at a time. For example, pianists, harpists, and players of mallet instruments play two staves at the same time. Therefore, for them it is better to learn to say the notes of one staff at a time.

Stringed or wind instrumentalists play from only one staff, so they have an easier time when learning to say notes. There is only one staff for them to think about. Organists read three staves, two for the hands, and one for the foot pedals. Then again, two organists playing together read six staves, and three organists read . . . Well, you understand, I'm sure. In any case, when learning to memorize by saying notes, say only one staff at a time and confine yourself to only a small number of notes.

If one measure has too many notes to remember, start with only half a measure.

Say the notes exactly in the rhythm that you would play them, with six-teenth notes in correct proportion to eighth notes, and so on. Keep looking back at the music to check for accuracy, and listen to the letters you say as you say the notes. You will soon discover that you can say whole *phrases* (a phrase in music means the same thing as it does in language arts—it's a complete musical thought) without even being near the instrument. Make sure you say the notes in rhythm.

If you are playing the organ, you might practice only the pedal line and say the notes of one hand. Then play the notes of the second hand and say the pedal notes, and of course, continue to read the music all the while you are saying the notes.

Then do the same exercise as above, only this time, don't look at the music. Just say and play without the music.

Analyze the Music

Completely analyze the music. Know what key the piece is in and what the key signature is. Take note of what material is repeated and what is new. Look for patterns of accompaniment and melody. Look for chords, inver-sions of chords, and arpeggiated patterns, and notice where they come in.

Count measures, and see how many times a melody or an accompanying figure repeats. There are often *phrases* that are repeated with only slight variations. If you learn what is the same and what is different in the music, the piece will be easier to understand and remember. You might even want to circle the difficult parts to remind yourself where extra work is needed.

Find Similarities, Differences

Learn those places that have patterns. Memorize the patterns, melody, or rhythmic lines that might be the same in several places in the music. Look at the music and find every place that is the same as another place and make mental note.

Find places that are similar but have small differences, and learn what the similarities are and what the differences are. Practice them alternating from one to the other.

A wonderful opportunity exists when two sections are the same but are written in different keys. Make sure you also memorize the lead-in notes for each of those sections.

When a melodic line is repeated several times in a piece there may be something slightly different each time it is repeated. If you learn not only the pattern but what is specifically different in each section, your memorization will be very conscious.

Practice Mentally

Play the piece in your mind without touching the instrument. See how far you can get. When you get stuck, look at the music and see what the next notes are. Then put the music away and try to play it in your head again. Eventually you'll be able to play right through the piece mentally without actually putting your fingers on the instrument. Incidentally, this kind of

practice is wonderful for any instrument or any discipline that requires study. Virtual practicing cuts through a lot of actual physical practicing and reinforces the brain's awareness of the piece.

I'm sure you've seen students "play" a piece by moving their fingers in their lap, in the air as if they were playing an air guitar, or on their arm as if they were playing the fingerboard of a violin. That's another way to practice without an instrument. It's very similar to mental practicing but adds a tactile element, whereas playing mentally without moving the fingers is more abstract and requires more conscious awareness.

One of the big advantages of practicing in your mind is that you can do it anywhere—while you're waiting in line, while you're in the shower, while you're combing your hair, even while you're driving a car. If people are watching you and shaking their heads to themselves, wondering what's wrong with you, you might want to leave this exercise until a time when there are less people around.

Another advantage to virtual practicing is that you can play the piece much faster in your mind than you can with your fingers, thereby finishing the piece much more quickly. Or you can leave out the parts you know well and only play those parts that you are not sure of. If you can, start playing from somewhere inside the piece instead of at the beginning. If you can't, then practice from different parts of the music until you can start from anywhere. Always remember to make many repetitions and to listen to every note you play as if you are listening to someone else.

Use Sleep to Help You Learn

Analyze, play, or work on the piece just before going to sleep. Often while you are sleeping your brain will continue to work on the passage you were concentrating on before you went to sleep, and you will find that when you waken you have a better understanding of it than you had before.

Listen to recordings of the piece you are working on played by various artists, and study the score while listening to the recording.

Put a pillow speaker under your pillow, and play the CD over and over while you sleep.

Write the Music Out

Writing the music out yourself is another good way to bring to the forefront every note that you must learn. With the printed music near you, try to write out part of a measure. Be sure to insert every marking that is in

the music, including dynamics, accents, and articulations. Then check your
work. Compare it to the printed page. If there are mistakes in what you
wrote, write it again, and, this time, correct the mistakes. Check it against
the printed page again. Keep doing this until you can write a few of the
measures absolutely correctly. If you memorize this way, you will soon
discover that you can write out whole sections of the piece completely by
memory, including every marking in the printed page. Eventually you'll be
able to write out a whole piece without missing one pencil stroke. (Incidentally, write in pencil, not pen, so that you can erase easily.)

Try to visualize in your mind what is on the printed page, page numbers,
parts of the music that might have a tear on it, coffee stains, or scotch tape.
Study the sheet carefully, and remember what the notes are around those
extraneous markings. Note where various chord changes are in the music.
Are they at the bottom of the page or at the top? Are they in the first measure of line three or line four? Try to make a mental picture of the music
that you can see in your mind. If you keep painting in parts of the music to
the picture in your mind, eventually you will actually see the entire score.
This is especially helpful when you have a memory lapse and all you have
to fall back on is the music in your mind.

Forgetting and Relearning on Purpose

In the beginning when learning how to memorize consciously, you
will forget the music. That's fine. Just rememorize it. Anything relearned
several times reinforces memory. It is actually better to allow the mind to
forget the music and then relearn it. Here's an idea: when you are trying to
consciously memorize something, after you've made many repetitions stop
that segment and go on to another segment.

As a matter of fact, try memorizing two different segments simultaneously (either from the same piece or different pieces), alternating from one
to the other. This forces the mind to forget one segment while working on
another. Don't do more than four measures in each segment, and do less
if necessary. Jump back and forth from one segment to the other. This way
you isolate the segments from the rest of the music and from each of the
pieces you are learning, and you learn each without having to get a running
start from an earlier part.

Another way to memorize consciously is to make many repetitions of one
part and then to stop looking at it for a half hour or so. Work on something
else altogether, and then go back to the part you were memorizing. Make
more repetitions. Again, allow the mind to forget, and then rememorize the

part. If you do this several times, you'll find you memorize sooner, better, easier, and more consciously.

Some Final Thoughts

Don't try to memorize (or even learn) an entire section of something in one sitting. It just won't happen, or, if it does, it's not going to be as good as if you were to keep going back to it. The more you look at something the more things you find out about it. In creating this book, I would write a while and then stop and move to something else I had to do. Several hours or a day later I would go back to the writing. When I reread what I had written, I realized it wasn't exactly what I wanted to say and needed to be modified, even though when I originally wrote it I thought it was exactly correct.

Always check what you have learned by looking back at the music. If you continue to consciously study the music while you are memorizing, every time you look at the music you'll discover something new, something you may not have noticed before, and each time you look, the music will become more a part of you.

Jump into the piece without prior practice from exactly the place you want to start (not at the beginning). How well you can play it is another way of telling you whether you know it or not. If you stumble, you don't know it. If you need to attempt several starts, you don't know it. If it goes smoothly and easily the first time, you know it.

Everyone can develop conscious memory skills, regardless of age or years of musical training. The techniques discussed in this chapter are not very difficult to learn, and they apply to everything. The more students work with them, the better they get. Used in combination, they are a powerful tool, one that will help students to learn and memorize easier, sooner, with less and less effort, not just music but *anything* requiring study. Conscious memory skills will help you retain whatever you are learning practically forever. Try it. I promise—you'll be very glad you did.

FOR INSTRUCTORS

There are at least three important components to education: learning, application, and retention of information. It is not enough to teach students how to learn something or how to practice it. Students must also learn how to memorize the material so that they can retain the information for long periods of time. All too often teachers hear the complaint of the student who works for months to learn a piece only to forget it two weeks after it is finished. This clearly indicates that something in the learning process is, at the very least, incomplete.

Many instructors are thorough and precise when it comes to teaching their students how to learn something but don't give them any instruction at all about how to memorize what they've learned. All too often they simply tell the student, "Great. You've finally learned this. That's terrific! Now go home and memorize it." When the moment comes for you, as an instructor, to tell the student to start working toward memorization, try to use some of the tips mentioned in this chapter. Don't just talk about them; spend some time to demonstrate how they work:

- Teach the student how to say notes and make her learn a half measure or a measure in rhythm in your presence so that she understands how to do it. As a matter of fact, assign the students to say notes as a homework exercise that you can listen to at the next lesson.
- Have the student write out a measure of the music in your presence. Make sure she includes all dynamics, articulations, and fingerings, if appropriate.
- Help the student analyze one or two measures of music identifying key signatures, chords, arpeggios, or anything that is significant in the measure.
- Choose a measure that is repeated somewhere else in the music and ask the student to find the repetitions.
- Have the student identify and be able to play portions of the piece where patterns, repetitions, and variations occur.
- Ask the student to play a section of music (not at the beginning); tell the student to stop at a particular place of your choosing, and ask her to point to the place in the music where she has stopped.
- Use the same exercise as above, and ask the student, without looking at the music, to identify the line and page number.

This is only a short list of the many ways to use the tips offered in this chapter. The more you can help the student understand the material, the sooner she will become consciously aware of what she is playing. To make the best use of this material, don't wait until it is time to memorize. If the student uses the ideas that I have talked about in this chapter from the moment she begins the piece, she will reduce the time it takes to learn, increase her understanding, and lengthen the amount of time she can keep the piece in her memory banks by many years.

POCO MOTO

Let's Get On with It

Music has charms to soothe a savage breast, to soften rocks, or bend a knotted oak.

—William Congreve, English playwright

PRELUDE

The man brought his two daughters to the instructor for an interview. "I want them to study piano," he said. He sounded adamant. The girls didn't look too happy.

The teacher turned to the two girls. "And what about you? What do you want to study?" she asked them.

They answered at the same time, almost as one voice. Without hesitation, they both said, "Flute."

The teacher asked the younger of the two girls, "Why flute?"

She answered, "Because it has a beautiful tone, like a silk ribbon. It's so pretty. I have lots of CDs with flute players. I want to play like that. I don't want the piano. I don't like the piano. I mean, it's okay, but I wouldn't want to learn to play it. I want to learn the flute."

The teacher turned to the other girl. "And you? Why do you want to study flute? Is it because your sister wants it?"

"No," she said. Then she continued, "But, my sister's right. The sound of the flute is sooo beautiful. Whenever I go to a concert, I always try to get my folks to sit near the flute section so I can hear it better and watch the flute players play. I know it's hard, but I want to learn flute so much. The piano is okay, but the flute is . . . I don't know how to explain it. The flute is just so much more beautiful. It has the most beautiful sound in the world."

Then the teacher turned to the father and said, "These girls want to study the flute, not the piano. Why are you trying to force them to learn the piano? They will do so much better at an instrument they like, and they obviously love the sound of the flute."

"I don't care what they want. Girls should study piano. It's better for them. If, after they study piano, they want to learn flute, then that's up to them. But first I want them to learn piano. That's it. No negotiation. If you won't teach them piano, I'll go somewhere else."

"Aw, please, Dad, let me study the flute first. Then after I can play the flute I promise I'll learn the piano if you still want me to," said the older girl. She tugged at her father's sleeve.

He was very determined and not at all impressed by the child's attempts to make him change his mind. "No," he said. "We talked about this, and I already told you: if you want music lessons, then you must study the piano first. Later you can learn whatever you want, but first you have to learn the piano. Everyone studies the piano first. That's it. I'm not going to argue with you."

The instructor looked at the father. "Excuse me, sir, but not everyone starts out in music with the piano. I'll admit the piano is a pretty popular instrument, but sometimes people start out with strings, or clarinet, or flute, or guitar. There is no hard and fast rule about it, and if the girls want the flute so much that they are willing to fight for it, don't you think, perhaps, it might be wise to give them a chance to—"

"No," he said, interrupting her in midsentence. "No, I don't, and I'm certainly not going to argue the point with you, either. I want them to learn piano first, and then, later, after they can play the piano, then we'll see. And if you don't want to take them, then we'll just have to go somewhere else."

The teacher answered, "Forcing students to take lessons in an instrument they don't want to learn is the fastest way I know to make them hate music and want to stop lessons. I just can't be a party to that. By all means, please take them somewhere else. And I predict that they won't take instruction very long."

Many years later, the older child, now an adult, was discussing taking flute lessons with a prospective instructor. She told the instructor, "When I was a girl, I wanted to learn to play the flute, but my father made me study the piano, and I hated it. It took me six months to convince him to stop my lessons. Of course, he never did let me learn the flute. From that time until now, I never stopped thinking about flute lessons. So, I went out and bought one, and here I am. Is it too late? Am I too old to start?"

The instructor smiled and said "No one is ever too old, and it certainly is never too late to begin music instruction, especially in an instrument you love. Welcome."

FOR EVERYONE

Practice Purposefully

If you want to turn three months of pointless practice into three weeks of work that results in accomplishment, always practice with a specific purpose in mind. Know beforehand what you want to learn, fix, or improve. Doing something again and again without having the brain involved is useless and wastes a lot of time. Years ago, there was a very popular adage: don't put the mouth in motion until the brain is in gear. The same goes for practicing. Don't put the fingers in motion unless the brain knows what the fingers have to do and is monitoring them. Think about student drivers. If they were to practice parallel parking without thinking about what they were doing, can you imagine how disastrous the results could be? Major, major fender benders.

A Case History

One day I heard trombone music coming from a practice room. Well, not exactly music—more like musical diarrhea. Someone was playing a very small passage of music over and over and over again. Every time the student played the little section, there was a mistake right in the middle of it—a hesitation between two notes where there should not have been any hesitation. No matter how many times the student repeated the section, I heard the same hesitation between the same two notes. It didn't get any better—not even a little bit. It just kept repeating itself again and again, exactly the same way.

Walking into the room, I asked the student, "What is the problem with the part you're practicing?"

"There isn't any problem. I always practice by repeating measures. That's how I learn it."

"But as I passed by, I heard you having some trouble. Here, look. It's right here." I showed her the place where she was hesitating between the notes and asked her if she heard it.

"No," she answered. "I never listen to what I'm playing. I just keep repeating it until my fingers learn it."

"But what if your fingers learn it wrong?"

She shrugged her shoulders. "Well, I guess I'll have to fix it later. First, the fingers have to learn to do it. For now, it's easier just to repeat it without thinking."

I sat down next to her. "That's what musicians call 'blind repetition.' You are doing repeats, but your brain isn't thinking, and your ears aren't listening. To fix something or learn something or make something better, you have to know *why* you're doing *what* you're doing. Besides being boring, blind repetition isn't productive. More often than not, without supervision from your brain and ears, the hands will make silly mistakes. That means they'll have to unlearn the mistakes first and then learn the part correctly. That takes twice as long. In your case, that's exactly what has happened. The hands are making a mistake right in the middle of the part you're practicing, and you weren't hearing it because you haven't been listening to what they are doing."

"I guess you're right," she said. "But that's the way I always do it. Maybe that's why it takes me so long to learn a piece. But that's the only way I know. What can I do to change it?"

"Let's try something," I said. I asked her to play it again and see if she could hear what was wrong.

Again she hesitated at the same spot. When she finished, she said, "I'm sorry—I still didn't hear anything wrong. Did I make the mistake again?"

"Yes," I answered. "Try it again, only this time, really, really listen, as if someone else is playing it."

Once again she played the section. This time she listened as she played. She even tilted her head toward the instrument. When she finished, she was very excited. "I heard it this time. I stop between those two little notes," she said, happily, pointing to the music.

"Good. Now you know what to listen for when you are practicing. Do it again, starting slower this time. Don't stop between those notes. Play it evenly."

This time it was perfect. "That's it. Now it's right," she laughed. "Thank you for helping me fix it."

"You're welcome, but it's not learned yet. It was only right this one time. That's like an accident. I wish we could learn things by doing it right just once, but the hands need to do it a lot more before you really can depend on them doing it right every time. Keep doing it at this speed until it is easy. Then, slowly increase the speed. It's going to take a few days and a lot of repetitions, but now you know what to listen for when you are practicing it. Remember, it's not enough just to play it over and over. You have to listen to what you do so that you hear when it is wrong *and* when it is right. If you don't listen for it, you can't hear it. If you don't hear it, you can't fix it. Now that you know how to fix it, you must do it again and again, making sure that every time you do it, it's correct. You have been playing it wrong for a long time. Now you must make it right more times than it has been wrong. Then, when you have done that, that's when it will be fixed for good."

Listening Is Crucial

There's a good lesson in that case history. If students want to cut days, weeks, and months from their learning time by making their practice more productive, they can't just practice by blind repetition. When they keep repeating a mistake, the ratio of right to wrong becomes inverted. They must listen to what they are doing, figure out what's wrong, and fix it so that there are more rights than wrongs. Blind repetition where students just keep repeating the same mistake during practice is useless.

In order to be able to hear what's wrong, the student must know what the section should sound like. If the student knows that, then she can listen to whether it is being played the way it is supposed to sound. If the music sounds a little off, that's a good clue that there is something wrong.

Hear What's Wrong, Make It Right

As an example, if someone tells you to spell the word *dog* and you spell it c-a-t, it doesn't matter how many times you spell it c-a-t; it will still be wrong unless you fix it. In order to fix it, you have to know that c-a-t is not the way to spell *dog*. You must know that in order to spell *dog* you need to write the letters d-o-g. You must know what those letters look like when they are written, you must know what the word *dog* looks like, and then you must consciously change the spelling of the word you wrote from c-a-t to d-o-g.

With music, it's the same thing. You must hear what's wrong. If you want a section to be even, you must hear a CD or someone play or something that shows you what it sounds like when it is even. You must recognize that your playing isn't even, and you must consciously work to make it even. If you want it to be soft, you must hear that it's not, and you must make it soft.

If you want to make sure the fourth finger crosses over the thumb smoothly so that there is no hesitation in the notes, you must hear the hesitation, you must hear it when it is without a hesitation, and you must make the fourth finger cross over the thumb smoothly.

So if you want to learn in a few weeks what it takes others months to accomplish, make sure you

- listen to find out what is wrong,
- listen to what it should sound like when it is played correctly,
- listen while you make repetitions to see if you are fixing what is wrong,
- choose different ways of making the repetitions to make practice more interesting, and
- remain focused and concentrated on what needs fixing.

FOR PARENTS

Parents often wonder how to make their children do more than just repeat notes without thought. They feel they are very lucky if they can get the child to agree to practice and repeat the parts that are wrong. They don't think too much about how to fix the part that is wrong, so long as the child continues to repeat it. They don't realize that saying "Let's do it five more times" doesn't mean and isn't the same as "Let's fix what's wrong with it, and then play it five more times correctly." As I said above, in order to fix a musical passage and to keep it fixed the student

- must recognize what is wrong in the first place,
- know what it is supposed to sound like when it is correct,
- fix what is wrong so that it is correct, and
- then repeat it enough times correctly to make it stick.

Believe it or not, there are ways to help young students become more aware of what they are doing when they are practicing. Following are just a few.

Record the Practice

Recording the passage provides a good way for the student to listen to the piece, because the student doesn't have to think about playing it at the same time she is listening. In addition, things don't sound quite the same if we are listening to a disc as when we are listening as we play, so it's easier to hear what the music really sounds like if we record it.

Therefore, ask the child to play the part and record it. Then, after it has been recorded, sit down with the child away from the instrument and listen to the disc together. Ask the child to tell you what's wrong when you come to the mistake. If the answer is, "Nothing—it's fine," perhaps you can point out the problem and have the child listen again and see if she can hear it.

Even a Young Child Can Be in Control

The hands won't do it by themselves. They can't. They need the student to tell them what to do and how to do it, and then the student must watch to see that they do it as they should. This is a little tough for a young child. However, if the child knows before she plays a section that she wants to hear the part played softly, or loudly, or whatever it is she wants to fix, there is a better chance that she can make it so. You, as a parent, can help your child do this. Before each set of repetitions, have the child say one thing she wants to fix. The little list below is just an example.

- "I want to make this really loud this time," and repeat the passage loudly five or ten times, listening to see if it is loud and clear;
- "I want to do it very evenly," and repeat it many times as evenly as possible; or
- "I want to make sure the fourth finger crosses over the thumb without any hesitation," and watch to make sure the fourth finger does just that.

Remember, in order to fix something the student must know what's wrong, must hear that it is wrong, must know what the piece sounds like when it is executed correctly, and then must make a conscious decision to make it right.

Make Repetitions with Thought

Sometimes knowing that something is wrong—even knowing what it is and how to fix it—is not the answer when helping a child practice. Sometimes the problem is first getting the child to make enough repetitions to learn to play the passage correctly. Let's say that your child is learning something and that her hands just can't do it yet. It's not a mistake; it's just a matter of developing the technique. That's one time when all that is needed is executing enough repetitions for the hands to achieve the technique.

In that case, the solution is simple: we must get the child to do enough repetitions to fix the passage and keep it fixed. There is a way to do this. If we keep changing the way we practice a tiny part, the repetitions add up quickly. Think about this: if a child repeats a passage

- five times slowly,
- five times very smoothly,
- five times in a very detached manner,
- five times very loudly, and
- five times very quickly,

in less than two minutes the child can do a whole lot of repetitions without even realizing it. What's more, she won't even feel it because every five times the child changes the way it is being played. She won't get a chance to get bored or annoyed at the practice. Do that several days in a row, and before you know it the passage is learned without any discomfort to the child.

Find the Hardest Parts, and Do Them First

Some parts are harder than others. Help the child to find the hardest parts and practice them first. There are often parts in a piece that the child can play easily, even when she is just learning them. Those aren't the parts that are going to need the most work. However, if the child happens to say, "Oh, I can't do this; it's just too hard," you have just identified the part to practice first. Take it slowly, practicing only a few notes. When the child feels success by fixing a teeny part of that hard section, she will be more willing to work further. If you can help the child fix the hard parts first, the easier parts will seem like a piece of cake.

In addition to what I have written in this section, there are a whole lot of ideas in the *For Students* section that you will be able to use to help your child practice more productively. You may have to modify some of them a bit, but, generally speaking, anything that works for older students will work in some form for children as well.

FOR STUDENTS

Productive Practice Rules

Here are some general rules for making sure that your practice is productive and not just blind repetition. I call them the Productive Practice Rules—PP Rules (and don't even think about going there!).

- Don't start from the beginning when you practice. I keep repeating this idea, but it is very important. Have you ever noticed that students always play the beginning of a piece better than the rest of it? That's because they play it more. Practice every part as much as you practice the beginning.
- Musicians must be able to consciously start from anywhere in the piece. Therefore, learn to jump around when you practice (in the music, not on your feet). Practice measures four through eight, and make many repetitions. Then practice measures fifteen through twenty with its repetitions. Then practice measures thirty-two through thirty-six, and so on. Just remember to also practice connecting measures, and don't play the measures just once or twice. Play them again and again and again.

Only Play through Twice

Whenever you practice, only play through the piece that you are working on twice—once at the beginning of the practice, to see what you need to do to make it better, and once at the end to see the improvement. *Playing through* something is just that—playing. Practicing is repeating small parts to learn, fix, or improve them.

Sometimes students think they know a piece but can actually only play it if they get a running start from an earlier part. For instance, they've practiced measures four through eight and can play the piece through from measures four through eight. However, when asked to play from measures five or six, they can't do it. That's because they don't consciously know what's in those measures. They simply don't know it. Working on each individual measure insures that we can start from anywhere—a big plus in case of a memory lapse.

Choose a really small part to practice, maybe only one measure. If that is too much to learn, start eliminating elements: practice a smaller amount of material; don't use dynamics; play it slower. There is always a point at which we can play something perfectly, even if it is very slow and only a few notes long. Find that point. It doesn't matter how short it is or how slow. That's the starting point. When you get to the moment that you can play even a teeny part correctly, you have determined how small a segment of the music to tackle at a time.

Remember that playing something on a musical instrument requires hundreds, sometimes thousands, of repetitions until the hands and the brain finally learn it automatically. The hands don't care whether those repetitions take two weeks, two months, or two years. Isn't it better to be able to learn something in two weeks rather than two years? By making many more repetitions than you think you should, you can accomplish a lot more in a lot less time. In addition, doing the repetitions purposefully and conscientiously reduces the total work required to learn the piece.

Don't Stop at the End of a Measure

Whenever you practice, never stop at the end of a measure, line, or beat. Always go to the first note of the next line, beat, or measure. That way you always know what is coming next.

Always Look and Think Ahead

When you are practicing, always look ahead. Train your eyes always to be a little ahead of the note or measure you are playing. In the beginning, it will be difficult to do, but as you get more and more used to it, looking ahead when you practice will become a natural thing for you to do.

Here's another idea: if you are working on music at a page turn, scotch tape the top of the line on the coming page to the bottom of the prior page so that you see the "present and future" on the same line and can therefore learn the transitions more easily.

It Takes Time

Never expect to learn something in an unreasonably short period of time. No matter how much or how hard you practice, it takes time for the body to absorb and be able to use the information learned. In addition to the body learning by productive, conscious practicing, the brain also learns as we sleep. During sleep the brain subconsciously works on the part that we struggled through during practice time. For that reason rehearsing right before bedtime is often very productive, in effect doubling the practice output—both as you practice the piece and as your mind processes the practice while you sleep. In chapter 10, I talked about using sleep to help you memorize. It works equally well to use sleep for learning without memorizing. No, I'm not kidding. It works. Try it.

Don't Just Fix One Note

When you play a wrong note, don't just stop, play the right note, and move on. That doesn't teach the hands anything. The reason you played the wrong note in the first place was because of something that *happened on the approach to that note*. That's what needs to be fixed. The hand must learn to approach the note differently. Whenever you make a mistake, back up to a few notes before the error occurred, start from there, pass through the place where you made the mistake, and play on until the first note of the next beat after the mistake. Repeat this process at least five times. That's the fastest and easiest way to learn how to play troubling segments correctly.

Read the Music

Continue to read the music and play by feel until you have learned everything that is on the printed page: the notes, rhythm, articulations, dynamics, tempo changes, or pedal markings. This is not about Learned Automatic Motion. Because we *can* play by feel while watching the music, that's the way we *should* play. Once students stop looking at the notation, there's nothing further they can discover in it. That little accent, a small crescendo mark, a *ritardando* (getting slower) sign, even a clef change can be lost forever if we stop looking at the music. Weeks after I had supposedly learned a piece I have discovered markings in the music that I had no idea were there.

Be Patient

There will only be a certain amount of improvement during any one practice session. We never completely learn or improve or fix something in one sitting, so we shouldn't expect that of ourselves. Be patient. Keep working at it.

Don't get frustrated if you practice hard but don't see immediate improvement. This is very common. Just stick with it. Sometimes it takes a combination of mental absorption, conscious practice, and learning during sleep to elicit a noticeable change. For a while nothing happens. Then, very suddenly, a few days or weeks later, when you've almost given up hope . . . Wow! What a difference!

We don't learn in a steady, smooth, upward progression like an escalator. Rather, there are many plateaus along the way, sometimes more than we'd like. Practice anyhow. Eventually we jump past the plateau to a new height. But doing so requires patience and perseverance.

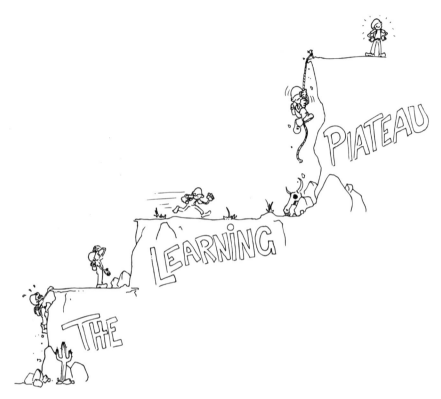

Overpracticing Can Be Dangerous

Overpracticing can hurt the hands. Professional musicians often get strains, tendonitis, and sore muscles, much like an athlete. Generally, intermediate and beginning students who are just playing a few hours a day don't practice strenuously enough to hurt their hands. However, if you do the same repetitive motion hour after hour and day after day, then you could injure your hands. Therefore, think about changing the touch or the hand or the part of the piece you practice every so often so that the motion is not too repetitive. Ideally students should have several pieces they are working on in varying stages of completion. A student might have one that is near to completion, one that is just being started, and one they're about halfway through. If you have at least three pieces from which to choose, it is easy to switch pieces so as not to strain the hand. Keep in mind that there are good pains and bad pains. When the muscles hurt because of a good workout, that's good pain. When the muscles get strained or sprained or when the insides of the arms hurt, those are bad pains. Students must know the difference and watch out for them.

Forget and Relearn

When your performance of a piece is riddled with bad habits, it's better to allow the hands and the mind to forget the piece entirely. Wait a few weeks or a few months, and then relearn it from scratch. You'll find that you learn it better.

Relearning something a second, third, or even fourth time is a good thing. Every time you learn it again you reinforce the memory and take the conscious understanding of the piece to a new level. However, be sure to allow yourself adequate time to forget it before relearning it.

Don't Tack On

Never tack on something you *don't* know to the end of something you already *do* know. Students tend to do this near the end of a piece, the end of a section, or the end of an assignment. They can play one part well, and they see that there are only eight measures left to learn until the end. They think to themselves, "Wow, I'm almost done." Instead of practicing the last part the same way they did all the other parts, they attach it to what they already know and try to play both parts together—only it doesn't work. The old part gallops along, and the new part sounds as if the poor horse is on its last legs. The new part never gets learned as well as the first part. Practicing this way wastes time and energy. Continuing small-measure practice right to the double bar is the quickest way to learn. Then when the last little part is as good as the rest it can be added in to the rest of the piece.

Review and Perform

Always review what you have already learned so as not to forget it. Too many students spend a lot of time learning something and then, because they never play it again, forget it within a few weeks after having finished it. The pleasure of learning music is in being able to play it. If after you can do it you don't do it, then what's the point? Therefore, a few times a week (not during practice time) sit down at the instrument and play for someone the pieces you already know. Play them for a family member; play them for friends; play them for your dog; play them for your hamster; play them for fun, for relaxation, for therapy, but play them. That way you develop a repertoire of pieces that you can play, anytime, anywhere, for anyone. You'll be surprised how quickly your repertoire grows. Just make sure that when you play music from your repertoire you play it as conscientiously and precisely as when you first learned it. If you don't, as I mentioned in the last chapter, you'll find that slowly the playing deteriorates and that within a short while you won't be able to play it at all.

Some Final Ideas

If some of the material in this chapter sounds like what I said in the chapter on developing memory skills, that's because these tips help in the learning as well as in the memorization process. Therefore, if you want to learn something faster, easier, with less stress, and with greater success, start using these tips as soon as you open a piece of music for the first time.

It is most important to remember that even when there seems to be no improvement whatsoever it is essential to practice nevertheless. When you are really, really tired after a long day, practice nevertheless. When you feel frustrated, isolated, and as if you are getting nowhere, practice nevertheless. Even when your progress feels nonexistent, practice nevertheless. You'll find that the joy of accomplishment is just around the corner.

FOR INSTRUCTORS

Teach Theory

Teaching the theory of music and abstract musical concepts is crucial to the progress of students, regardless of their age. Instructors sometimes feel that if students are very young it is easier to teach them to play first and then later to introduce theoretic concepts. In other cases, older students may not be interested in learning theory because they want to play and don't see the connection between theory and performance or between music and other aspects of their lives.

Granted, it is difficult for a private music instructor who teaches a student only one hour or one half hour once a week to incorporate theory into the lesson format. We start out with two strikes against us: First, whatever time we spend on theory takes that much time from the playing part of the lesson. Second, because we cannot spend more than five or ten minutes of a lesson on theory the student doesn't learn very much at any one time. Because there is so little time we often restrict ourselves to the most basic theory—notes, time values, intervals, chords, scales—and only relate them to music. We seldom show or even talk about the relationship of music to language arts, social studies, science, or mathematics.

It is much easier to teach theory in classroom situations where entire periods are available for explaining, discussing, and analyzing abstract musical concepts as an isolated subject apart from the element of performance.

Nevertheless, we must persevere and teach some theory during *every* lesson. The more we can help students make connections from music to various aspects of their lives, the easier it will be to keep them tuned in and turned on to music.

Relate Abstract Musical Ideas to Life

The more we can interest a student in abstract musical ideas and relate them to familiar subjects the easier it will be to teach performance. If a student understands that

- a phrase in music is the same as a phrase in English,
- a *motive* in music is the same as a molecule in science,
- two-sixteenths equals one-eighth in music, just as it does in mathematics,
- an interval in music refers to the distance between two places in music just as it does in language arts, and
- knowing the history of a composition, who wrote it, when it was written, why it was written, and what was going on in the country, in the area, or in the world at that time correlates music and social studies,

then that student will find it easier to coordinate the information she learns in music with information in other subjects she already understands.

It's Not Enough to Play the Instrument

It is simply not enough for students to be able to play their instruments. At the very least, the students of private music instructors should be capable of passing examinations based on the criteria found in The National Standards for Arts Education. Instructors should have juries, examinations, evaluations, and opportunities for solo and group performances. When possible, instructors should invite students to hear, see, and take part in lectures, programs, and various musical performances, some of which might be unfamiliar and outside of the students' comfort zones.

Look at the National Standards

The website http://artsedge.kennedy-center.org/teach/standards/contents .cfm lists achievement standards for k–12 classroom music students as well as levels for students in other art forms, including dance, theater, and visual arts. These standards are relevant to students of private music instructors as well.

Basic Rules

Students should work from an assigned age-appropriate theory book. Lessons should include not just standard theory but also tidbits of history; information about the relationship of psychology and other sciences to music; pattern development in music, art, science, and mathematics; form and analysis; and information about various instruments. The assignments should include biographical and historical projects; opportunities for the student to create her own music, arranging, and orchestration; and any other elements that enrich their understanding of the world of music.

Many instructors work from theory notes that they themselves have developed. That's good also. However, don't offer paper handouts to students. The quickest way to make sure important reference materials get torn, destroyed, or eaten by the dog is to hand them to your student, piece by loose-leaf piece. If you have a lot of these papers, make a bound booklet from them, and hand *that* to the student. There's a better chance that a booklet will last longer than a lone piece of paper.

Incidentally, the above Kennedy Center website has hundreds of projects, lessons, ideas, and achievement goals from which music instructors can draw to help students develop an interest, an involvement, and a connection to all aspects of their instruction. Playing the instrument should be only the first spoke in the wheel of music education.

GRADUS AD PARNASSUM

Seven Days to Success

Music washes away from the soul the dust of everyday life.

—Red Auerbach, football coach

PRELUDE

When Jordan arrived at his lesson, he was very annoyed. He said to his teacher, "You can't have any idea of how frustrated I am. I practiced this one page just the way you told me to, many, many times, in really small sections. I must have spent two or three hours on Monday working on it. I did it loud and soft, fast and slow, hands together, and hands separately. Really, I was at it so long that even my wife complained. Finally, after I don't know how long, I got it. It was clean. Every note was right. The rhythm was correct. There were no hesitations, and I really felt like I had accomplished something. As you suggested, even after I got it, I kept playing it to make sure it would stay in my fingers. It was really good."

"That's wonderful. I'm really glad. Good for you," said Mr. Alexander. "So what's the problem?"

"That was Monday. On Tuesday, I opened the music I had practiced Monday first, figuring I'd have a little fun playing something that had finally gone so well the day before. Guess what? My fingers couldn't even find the notes. It was like I never saw the piece before. I remembered what you said about patience, so I practiced it again and relearned the whole thing. By the time I closed the book, I could play it quite well, and my initial frustration disappeared. I really felt much better."

Mr. Alexander smiled. "That's great. So what's wrong? Why are you so upset now? I don't understand."

"Because, frankly, I've had it with practicing. I am now convinced I just can't learn, even practicing the way you said. I did it your way, and it didn't happen."

"What do you mean, 'it didn't happen'?" asked Mr. Alexander. "You just told me that it did."

Jordan put up his hand as if to ask for silence. "Please," he said, "you haven't heard the end of the story. Again on Wednesday I started my practice with the same piece. After all that work Monday and Tuesday I felt pretty confident on Wednesday. But when I tried, I still couldn't play it. Again, I remembered your pep talk about needing several days of consecutive work, and so I relearned it again. Finally, I could play it easily many times. When I left practice on Wednesday, I was sure I had it. Now we come to Thursday. You're not going to believe this, but I tell you honestly, my fingers hadn't retained zip from the three days of practice before. Nothing. Zilch. I couldn't do it. I just couldn't do it. It was like those three days of practice never existed.

"I realized then that it's time to give up. It's not worth the trouble. I'll never be able to do this. Maybe I'm just not cut out for playing music. How long does it take to learn one lousy page in a piece, anyway? I could be at this for years before I get anywhere with it."

Mr. Alexander nodded his head and smiled. "Oh, now, I understand," he said, "and I really do have the answer for you, if you want to hear it."

"Of course I do! But, truthfully, maybe I'm just too old to learn, or too slow or too . . . I don't know too *what*, but I'm definitely too *something*."

"No, you aren't. You just didn't know that it would take more days to get it than you anticipated. You really were on the right track. Your practicing was great, and you did exactly what you should have done."

"Evidently not," answered Jordan, dejectedly.

"Yes, you did. Just hear me out. Everything you did was absolutely correct. You worked on it the first day until you could play it with some facility. You practiced it until you really had it. Then the following day you relearned it, starting from scratch again. And the third day, when you still couldn't do it, you relearned it again."

"Yes, I did, but the day after that I still couldn't play it," argued Jordan.

"Jordan, do you remember what I told you about practice, that no one can learn something so that it sticks after just a couple of practice sessions? I said one or two days of learning wouldn't put it in your fingers and in your head forever; it would need about seven days to make it really solid."

"Yes, so I did exactly what you said, and it didn't work. After three days of really careful practice, on the fourth day I still couldn't play it."

"It takes longer. It needs about a week, sometimes a little longer, until the brain and the fingers can really feel that the section is learned. Until you do that much work on it, it's just not going to stay. Everything you did was correct. You just didn't do it long enough. A few more days and you would have had a wonderful success."

"Are you saying I just didn't keep working on it long enough?"

"That's it. A few more days and it would have been yours."

"Okay. I'll tell you what. I really want to see if your system works. I'm going to go home, and I'm going to do this page for another week. I'm gonna do everything you said. I really want to see if you're right."

"I can promise you that if you continue to practice the way you have been for another few days, by next lesson you'll be so comfortable playing it that you won't even remember today's conversation. Let's call this a challenge. How about it?"

"Okay; you got it. But if next week . . ."

"You don't even have to worry about it. I promise."

FOR EVERYONE

Day after Day

It is very important to remember that nothing is learned in a day. Regardless of how short a piece is, how small a part a student tackles, or how easy the piece might seem, repeated practice is essential, day after day after dismal day, until finally we can say we own the piece (until it's effortless to play and doesn't require much conscious thought.) Remember, we (and I count myself among the we's) can't say it's ours—that we own it—until we can play it easily. It is not enough to be able to struggle through something, worrying all the while about whether or not we can get through it without some kind of disaster occurring along the way. It has to feel good in the fingers. We have to be able to play it comfortably and naturally so that during the playing we can think about the other things that we need to do to make the music sound beautiful.

A Seven-Days-to-Success Plan

In prior chapters I have offered a lot of general suggestions for how to practice more productively. This chapter deals with a seven-days-to-success program: a specific plan that will help students improve, fix, or learn whatever material the instructor assigns during a lesson, so that by the following week's session, performance of the piece will be noticeably better. No more excuses! No more "I tried, but I just couldn't learn it." All the student has to do is follow this plan, and within a week, give or take a day, the assigned sections of music will be very much improved.

Cramming Doesn't Work

Beginning and early intermediate students often try to learn assigned sections of a musical composition by laboriously plodding their way through the entire thing in one or two practice sessions. That method just doesn't work. It is rather like cramming for a big examination at the last minute. Think back to the days when you were still in school. Come on, now, be honest—how much did you *really* learn when you waited until the night before a big test to study? Not a whole lot, I'll bet.

Using the Seven-Days-to-Success Plan

The better idea is to learn something little by little in a structured, systematic manner. The seven-days-to-success plan does just that, but students have to stick with it. It won't be easy. The biggest problem that beginning and intermediate students have is that they start out gung ho with every new project, piece, or assignment but, little by little, lose steam long before they complete the job. (Incidentally, did you know that the phrase *gung-ho* comes from the Mandarin Chinese *gonghe* and is a standard abbreviation for *gongye hezuoshe*, meaning "industrial worker's cooperative"? What's that? You didn't know? Well, now you do. It's probably more information than you needed, but if you are *really* interested in knowing how the phrase *gung-ho* crept into the English language, check out the glossary at the back of this book.)

It Works for Everyone

Anyway, this seven-day plan requires focus and perseverance, but it really works for both adults and children. Sure, there will be some frustration along the way, but success is practically guaranteed if students stay with it. What's more, with a little modification this program works for learning anything, not just music. It is even a good way to study for a test. Because it spreads out the learning over a longer period of time, it is less stressful; the mind retains the information longer and, in the case of playing an instrument, so do the fingers.

FOR PARENTS

Please study the instructions below carefully. Although the seven-days-to-success plan may sound like it is complicated, it really isn't. One modification may be necessary, however, when you work with a youngster. Because of the attention span and limited perseverance of the child, think about shortening the length of the passage the student works on. Instead of one measure at a time, practice only half a measure. In that way the child achieves little successes sooner. Help the child make a game of it, and keep score of how many correct repetitions he makes.

FOR STUDENTS

The Seven-Days-to-Success Plan

Day One   Find the first four measures in the assignment. You'll probably be able to learn those four measures in about a half hour. Are you ready? Here's how: First divide the four-measure section into four one-measure segments. Practice note one of measure one to note one of measure two until it is absolutely correct and smooth. If there are too many notes in the first measure, then practice only half a measure at a time. If there is only one note in a measure, then make the segment two measures long. In any event, whatever part you practice should be played with a good tone. It can't sound like mouse music. That is, the notes, the rhythm, and the fingering must be precise, and there can't be any hesitation.

You'll have to do it many times before you can finally play it correctly, because you will make mistakes along the way. At the slightest slip-up, stop immediately, because whatever you do after the mistake is no longer useful. Once the passage is correct and smooth, you must play it absolutely perfectly six times. Keep score. After you get it right the first time, you may mess it up again on the next round and maybe several rounds after that. That's okay. The six perfect repetitions don't have to be consecutive, but count only the ones that are correct. Don't count anything that has a mistake in it. As you get more and more confident in the playing of the measure, you'll probably do it a little faster each time. That's okay. Just be careful not to play it too fast, or you will lose control of it.

When the first measure is learned, start with measure two, and go to the first note of measure three. Do the same thing as you did in measure one. Go back to the original speed. Don't try to learn the new measure at the same speed you were at when you finished practicing the first measure.

After measure two is successful, join both measures together. Start at note one of measure one, and go to note one of measure three. The same rules apply. You must make six perfect repetitions. Warning: practicing a larger section (even though you already learned both measures) makes it harder. Therefore, start these repetitions much more slowly and thoughtfully.

After you have made six perfect repetitions of measures one and two, begin on measure three, and go to note one of measure four. Practice the same way. We need six faultless playings. Remember, don't count repetitions that have mistakes in them (even teeny errors), and don't continue playing after you have made a mistake. Whenever there is a mistake, stop, and start again from the beginning of measure three.

When measure three is learned, go back to the beginning of measure two, and practice through the first note of measure four. Be especially careful when you add another measure. If there are more measures, it's more complicated and therefore harder to make it correct. Practice slowly. Remember that the repetition only counts if it's absolutely correct.

After having put measures two and three together, learn measure four to note one of measure five the same way. Be careful—don't let the practice get sloppy.

Okay, so now you've practiced and made six perfect repetitions of each individual measure from measure one all the way to note one of measure five, and you've joined two of the measures. Now we are going to work backward. Put measures three and four together to note one of measure five. Yes, you still have to do six perfect repetitions. Remember to start each set of repetitions slowly.

When measures three and four are done, start from measure two, and go to note one of measure five. By this time you're probably getting tired of making all these repetitions (and making so many mistakes before they become correct), so my advice is this: with each repetition play a bit more slowly than the last, and watch every note. If you really watch everything and play very carefully, you may even be able to make some of the countable repetitions consecutively.

When you have completed six perfect repetitions of measure two through note one of measure five, go back one more measure (that's right, to the beginning of the assignment). Start at note one of measure one, and go and go all the way to note one of measure five. Play it really slowly, and try to make as many perfect repetitions as possible, one after the other. When you have completed six repetitions perfectly, close the book! You're done. For the first day, anyway!

Day Two   Uh-oh. Bad news. You won't be able to play the part you practiced so hard yesterday, at all. It's going to feel like you never practiced it at all. You will have to start the section all over again. That's okay. Be patient. Shake off the frustration and start from scratch.

Relearn it as you did yesterday, one measure at a time. Remember that we need six perfect repetitions. Always go to note one of the next measure. Practice slowly, and count only the repetitions that are perfect. I know that it will be annoying, but ignore the irritation, and just press on.

Surprise, surprise. You'll find that within a few minutes you'll be able to play each individual measure correctly, and you will achieve the six required repetitions a good deal faster than yesterday. Don't combine measures until you have completed the six perfect repetitions of each individual measure.

When you have relearned all six measures, begin combining two measures plus one note. Start at measure one, and go to the first note of measure three. Practice slowly, and make your repetitions.

Then combine measures two and three to note one of measure four. Make your repetitions. Then join measures three and four to note one of measure five, and do the same thing.

Now start again at measure one, and practice measures one, two, and three all the way to note one of measure four. Make your repetitions. By this time, you should be noticing that the playing is coming easier and that you no longer struggle as much. That *is* happening, isn't it? Good.

When you have successfully completed your repetitions of measures one to note one of measure four, start at measure two, and go to note one of measure five. Do the same thing.

Finally, play all four measures through to note one of measure five. Make the repetitions. By this time this part should be as good as and probably better than it was yesterday. And I bet it took less than half the time that it took yesterday. Now, that wasn't so hard, was it? And you still have time left from your half hour, don't you?

Okay, now, let's take the next two measures from the assignment. Work on those the same way you did yesterday, in the first segment. Practice individual measures plus one note until you can do six perfect repetitions. Then combine them. Since the two new measures immediately follow the older segment, you will have to join them to that part by practicing measures four and five to note one of measure six and measures five and six to note one of measure seven as well. Don't choose more than you can work on in the same time frame as you did yesterday. Make sure that the repetitions are just as precise as those you made in the first segment.

Today's practice in the first segment probably took only about ten or fifteen minutes. That leaves you an equal amount of time to work on the new part. After you have learned the new part and joined it to the old part, close the book and go on to something else. There, now. Doesn't that make you feel as if you have accomplished something?

Day Three   Bad news! Very bad news! Brace yourself. You're not going to be a happy camper. When you try the first segment for the first time today, you still won't be able to do it. It will be just as weak as when you started it on day one. I know how frustrated you must be. Shh—be courageous. It's all part of the plan. This is the way we learn it. Don't worry.

Start from scratch—again! Only this time, start backward. Work on measure four to note one of measure five first. Then do measure three, and so on, all the way back to measure one. After about two or three times, you'll see—the individual measures will come back together. Remember to make your repetitions, only today make five repetitions instead of six.

See? You did it, didn't you? Now try two measures at a time. You should find that the two-measure segments also come back together after a few tries. Don't forget to always go to note one of the next measure. Then do three measures. Remember to play slowly and to always overlap the measures. (Practice a measure of the part you know, and join it to a measure of the part you don't know. Play measures one and two, two and three, and three and four.) Make five repetitions after you can play each segment easily. Within just a few minutes I'll bet the earliest section will be fine—even better than it was yesterday.

Now go on to the newer part, and relearn that, individual measures first, just as you did yesterday. Then go to two-measure groups. (Since there are only two new measures, it shouldn't take long.) Okay now, join segment two to segment one. Hmm, not bad, right? You really *can* do it. Remember to make six perfect repetitions of the new part and five repetitions of the old part. It's beginning to go much more smoothly now, isn't it? And it has hardly taken any time at all. You will probably even have a few minutes from the original allotted half hour to work on a new section.

So check out the next two measures, and practice them the same way as you did the first segment on the first day. After you have made six perfect repetitions of the third segment, attach measure six to measure seven and measure seven to measure eight. Don't just tack it on. Join it by practicing *only* measures six and seven to note one of measure eight and only measures seven and eight to note one of measure nine. Remember to overlap all measures, practice slowly, and, each time you add another element, begin at the slower speed again.

Day Four   When you begin today's practice on the oldest part, you still won't be able to do it on the first shot. Relax! Don't get upset. In a few minutes you'll be able to do it. I promise. Watch what will happen. Here we go.

Start again, and relearn it just as you did yesterday. It comes together very quickly, now, doesn't it? I bet in just a few minutes the first and second parts will be smooth and easy. Now, go to the third part. Relearn that. Then join it to the second and first parts, remembering to start it slower each time you add another element. And today do four perfect repetitions of parts one and two and six of part three.

After all that, I bet you have enough time left from the allotted half hour to start another two measures. Remember to do it exactly the same way as you did all the other measures.

Day Five   Almost there, aren't you? It looks like it's beginning to take shape, doesn't it? Maybe just one or two little mistakes in the notes of the first part, the first couple of times.

Try it again slowly, carefully, and I bet on the second or third try you'll be able to do the first part without a hitch. Make three beautiful repetitions. Now go to the second part, but start at measure four so that you have continuity from one part to the next. This one isn't quite as easy as the first part, but it's pretty good, right? Five or six tries and you can do it, can't you? Remember the repetitions.

When you've relearned the second part, try the third part. Don't get discouraged if all the parts you've been working on seem to be on different plateaus. Because you have been practicing each of them a different number of days, some are better than others. That's okay. If there is a serious difference in their levels, then don't join the segments just yet. Maybe wait until tomorrow. In the meantime, just keep doing the measure groups. Better make four repetitions of the third segment today.

Day Six Hopefully, today is the day that you should be able to get through the earliest part correctly on the first or second try. Come on. Let's give it a go. Just do the first part. There! Doesn't that make you feel good? And just in case you can't, repeat the first part one or two times, and you'll be able to do it. All the other parts are improving also. If you keep working on them the same way you practiced the first part, within a few days you'll have all of those learned too.

Do you remember what I said at the beginning of this chapter? If you use this seven-day plan to practice, by your next lesson you will be playing the assignment noticeably better than you did at last week's lesson. Tomorrow when you see your instructor you will be able to demonstrate exactly that. I hope that you recognize the excellent progress you have made on this assignment.

Day Seven I bet today you had a wonderful lesson, maybe the best lesson ever. Okay, maybe there was a slip-up or two, but they were due to nervousness, not lack of practice. In general you not only demonstrated how well this plan works, you also demonstrated how well you worked through it. Remember this phrase (you should say it before and after every practice session): Yes, I can; yes, I can; yes, I most definitely can!

Summary The seven-days-to-success plan is simple, but you must stick with it. Let's summarize:

- Be patient. Keep at it. Don't get discouraged if it's not better even after you practiced it well the day before.
- Practice each segment six consecutive days (at least), and maybe even more.
- Practice individual measures, then two measures at a time. Overlap measures.
- Repeat them until you can play them correctly.
- Make six perfect repetitions. Don't count any repetitions where there is the slightest mistake. When it is finished, it should feel smooth and easy.
- Every day relearn each group of measures from scratch, as if it were the first day.
- Increase the speed with each correct repetition.
- When you add another element (like another measure), begin at the slower speed.
- As each part gets a little better, add another section—a measure or two more.
- Overlap the measures you are working on for continuity.

- Don't tack on a part you don't know as well to a part you already know.
- Knowing the part well means being able to play it correctly, smoothly, and easily.
- Expect to plateau between various sections. Sometimes it just doesn't seem to get better for a while. Don't be discouraged when that happens. Just keep working at it. Things will get better. I promise.

FOR INSTRUCTORS

One of the biggest problems that instructors have is making sure that students practice productively. During the lesson most instructors carefully explain to their students exactly what to do at home, but by the time the student is ready to sit down and practice he has forgotten most of what the instructor said and must rely on whatever instructions are written in the assignment book and whatever the student has remembered from the lesson. Because instructors spend the majority of the lesson teaching, there usually isn't time at the end of the hour to write more than a short to-do list in the assignment book, very limited minimal how-to's, and practically no whys or what-to-watch-fors.

To achieve the best results from practice, it is very important that the student knows exactly what to do, how to do it, and especially what problems will occur (which will lead to annoyance, irritation, and frustration) during the days in between the lessons. Much of the frustration that students experience during practice erupts because even though instructors warn them, students are not sufficiently informed about what to expect and therefore are not prepared to deal with difficulties that arise.

I have created the seven-days-to-success plan in order to fill in the gap between what instructors tell the students at the lesson and what happens during practice in the week between lessons. The purpose of the seven-days-to-success plan is fourfold:

- to help students know what to do at home and precisely how to do it,
- to help students expect, and be aware of, all the potentially irritating problems that will occur during practice between lessons,
- to help students be prepared for and deal with those problems in a constructive manner, and
- to teach students how to work through an assignment, so that some noticeable improvement is achieved from one lesson to another.

Encourage your students to pay particular attention to this chapter. Make sure they become very familiar with what they can accomplish from lesson to lesson if they follow the plan. You might want to hold a group meeting at which you can discuss the seven-days-to-success plan with all your students and parents. In addition, you might want to make posters to hang in your studio that describe the plan and describe each day separately.

Keep in mind that the students who practice two hours a day will be able to accomplish more in seven days using this plan than those who practice only one hour or half an hour. When you assign work to your students, try to find out how long they practice (without focusing on time), and make sure that the amount of work you assign fits into the amount of time they can practice. Don't assign more than is possible for students to accomplish in the time they have available. Make sure you become totally familiar with where a student should be in his practice on each day, and encourage students to call you, if at the end of a particular day, they have special frustrations. And of course remember that the plan is only an approximation and will need to be individually adjusted for each student. Emphasize to your students that if they really know, understand, and use this plan in their practice, the improvement they make from week to week will not just be noticeable, it will be outstanding.

13

AL PERFEZIONE
Scales, Arpeggios, and Chords

Scales played in the correct musical way are very exciting and rewarding.

—James Galway, flutist

PRELUDE

"Please explain the nature of your complaint."

"Yes, your honor. It's like this. My next door neighbor is a piano student. His house is close to mine, too close, and I hear him practice piano at all hours of the day and night. Eleven o'clock in the morning, nine o'clock at night, two o'clock in the morning, four o'clock in the afternoon. It goes on for hours and hours. It never stops! I can even tell when he isn't there because that's the only time I don't hear him practicing. It drives me crazy. Sometimes he sounds like my granddaughter when he plays. My eight-year-old granddaughter practices the same things as he does. She calls them scales. Only she practices them a few minutes and goes on to other things. Not him. He practices the same stuff for hours. I can hear those scales in my sleep."

"He never practices anything else?"

"Oh, yes, your honor, sometimes he does, but even when he plays something else he repeats little teeny parts of it the same way over and over and over again. Sometimes he repeats six or seven notes so many times that it

makes me want to scream. He never plays anything through; he just practices little parts. Your honor, I'm going nuts. Really. I'm not kidding. I can't
take it anymore.

"Once in a while he starts to play something that actually sounds nice,
even to me with my tin ear, and I think to myself, Boy, I could listen to
this! But it doesn't last more than twenty seconds, and then he's off again,
practicing something else with his thousand and ten repetitions."

"Can't you go to another part of the house while he practices?"

"I'm sorry, your honor, but it's impossible. It's so loud and so annoying
that you can't escape it anywhere. We can hear it all over the house. There's
no place I can go to get away from it. And I'm talking hours—five, six, seven
hours at a time. He has no mercy. The only time I have any peace is when
he is away. And I know it seems unfair, because he is away a lot of the time,
weeks and weeks, sometimes even months. But just as I begin to get accustomed to the quiet and I relax a little, he comes back, and it starts all over
again. There is just no end to it when he is here. Your honor, please—you
really have to do something to help me."

"Sir, do you know who your neighbor is?"

"No, sir. I've never really met him. Actually, I've never even seen him.
I've seen his wife come and go from time to time, but not him. All I know
about him is that he's a Russian gentleman and that he plays the piano like
my eight-year-old granddaughter. Please, your honor, I don't care who he
is. You've got to make him stop."

"Sir, your neighbor is Maestro Vladimir Horowitz, one of the greatest
concert pianists of the twentieth century. He performs all over the world.
You should consider yourself very fortunate that you can hear him play in
such an informal setting. People pay hundreds, sometimes thousands, of
dollars to hear him play in concert."

"Your honor, that may be true, but if they lived next door to him and
heard him practice the same thing over and over and over like I do, they'd
ask for their money back."

FOR EVERYONE

Everyone who studies a pitched musical instrument (an instrument that
makes many different sounds) must eventually learn to play scales, arpeggios, and chords (I call them SACs, and they have no relation at all to the
academic SATs). Everyone who learns the SACs—hates them. Come to

think of it, students don't like the SATs either, so maybe there *is* a relationship of some kind.

Most students consider scales, arpeggios, and chords to be the most boring, annoying, and monotonous of all exercises. No one enjoys practicing them, especially not those in the beginning or intermediate stages of their music instruction. However, the fact remains that even though most students don't understand them and certainly don't appreciate their worth, scales, arpeggios, and chords—SACs—are, nevertheless, among the most valuable tools available to anyone who really wants to become proficient at his musical instrument.

What Is a Scale?

Before we go ahead, let's define *scale*. We are not talking about the kind of scale you use to weigh vegetables or yourself, and it isn't anything like the skin on a fish either. A scale in music is sort of like an escalator that gradually goes up and down by degrees. To musicians, a scale is a series of notes comprised of all or most of the letters of the musical alphabet (A, B, C, D, E, F, G), which we play in order, in a stepwise ascending or descending pattern. When we play the letters forward (from A up to G), the tones go higher. When we play them backward (from G down to A), the tones go lower. There are many kinds of scales: major, minor, whole tone, pentatonic, blues, and others. Beginning and intermediate students generally study the major and minor scales first.

In some places in the world instead of using the ABCDEFG letter names, musicians call the notes do, re, mi, fa, sol, la, and ti. In the 1965 musical film *The Sound of Music*, Rogers and Hammerstein (the composer and lyricist) made scales famous in their song called "Do-Re-Mi." The words went like this:

> Doe, a deer, a female deer,
> Ray, a drop of golden sun,
> Me, a name I call myself,
> Far, a long, long way to run.
> Sew, a needle pulling thread . . .

And so on.

Of course they took a little liberty with the words, but you get the idea. People all over the world claim the syllables do, re, mi, and the rest come from the language of whatever country they live in. Spanish-speaking people will tell you the syllables are Spanish words. Italians claim they are Italian. French folks will say they are French. Actually, they are just *syllables* (the first part of words) taken from a Latin hymn, but that's a story for another time and another book.

What's an Arpeggio?

The Italian word *arpeggio* means *like a harp*. *Arpeggiated* patterns mean that we skip at least one letter in between each two notes we play. Generally speaking, an arpeggio is the first, third, and fifth notes of any scale, played one note at a time—A C E A C E A C E A C E—in some kind of rotating or continuing sequence. And we can play them forward or backward (up and down) just as we can with the scale.

What's a Chord?

When we play those same three arpeggio notes at the same time, we call that a *chord* or a *triad* (think in threes: *tri*ad, three notes; *tri*cycle, three wheels; *tri*angle, three angles; *tri*pod, three legs; and *tri*fecta—oops. That's a horse of a different color.

Although we often use the words interchangeably, there actually is a difference between a *chord* and a *triad*. A triad is the first, third, and fifth note of any scale played together, or as close together as we can. A chord, on the other hand, is any bunch of notes but at least three played at the same time. Therefore, a triad is always a chord, but a chord is not always a triad. By the way, a chord is not the same thing as a cord. Note that the musical chord is spelled with an *h*; the cord with which you tie a package doesn't have an *h*.

A little trivia here: singers have vocal cords. (Actually, so do those folks who can't sing.) In spite of the fact that they use their vocal cords for something musical, what they have in their throats are cords, not chords.

Incidentally, singing triads is really hard to do unless you have three mouths or three singers, each singing one note, or two singers, one of whom has two mouths. In any event, in the case of singers each mouth can sing only one note at a time, unless of course you mix the sounds electronically. (That's a good way to give someone a real shock.)

Woodwind and brass players also can only play one note at a time, and therefore they can't play chords either, at least not if they are playing a solo. Of course if they play together, each instrumentalist can play one note. And you know what people say: those who play together stay together.

SACs Are Everywhere in Music

Anyway, let's talk about these irritating, nonmusical exercises that every-body hates. Why should students or anyone practice scales, arpeggios, and chords? Why not just learn the technique needed to play each piece indi-vidually? To most students just starting out, learning how to play something you can actually perform for someone seems more logical than practicing exercises that are just that—exercises. After all, no one is ever going to play only scales, arpeggios, or chords in a concert. *Or are they?*

The fact remains that everyone plays SACs in music all the time; they just don't realize it. All music—everything we play or sing—is made up of scale, arpeggio, or chord patterns or a combination of all three, simply because there are no other possibilities in music. Yep, it's true. That's the way music is composed. Sorry about that.

Since all music is patterned in scales, arpeggios, or chords, if we can ex-ecute all the SACs in every imaginable configuration perfectly all over our instrument, our fingers will learn to gravitate to the notes that we must play in those configurations automatically.

SAC Technique Transfers to Pieces

Even more important, the technique learned in the study of scales, ar-peggios, and chords automatically transfers to every piece we play or sing in that configuration with very little extra practice. That's what makes SACs so valuable, important, and wonderful. Being fluent in the SACs trims years off the learning process, because it eliminates a great deal of practice that would otherwise be spent learning individual pieces. A student who has carefully and correctly practiced the SACs in every configuration on his instrument will recognize those patterns in the music and will immediately and automatically be able to play those passages.

Let's see how this works when a student is learning a piece. Say you no-tice that the notes in a piece of written music that you are learning actually comprise a scale. You also see that the fingering in the music is the same as in the scale. Studying a little further, you discover that the scale is spread out over a four-measure section and that it goes up and down, up and down. If all the notes are exactly the same as in the scale, that's four measures you don't have to bother practicing. Even if there are a couple of changes from the original scale, by looking for only what's different you can learn the pas-sage relatively quickly without having to spend hours working with it as if it were something completely new. Even though it *is* a new section of the piece you are learning, it is material you are already familiar with through the study of the SACs.

Benefits of Practicing SACs

Careful practice of scales, arpeggios, and chords teaches musicians how to do certain things automatically, without thinking. There's that word again, *automatically*. Yes, I'm referring to the Learned Automatic Motion (LAM) that I spoke about in earlier chapters. This is LAM at its best. Here's a short list of what the SACs teach:

- how to hold the arm in order to make a thumb turn most efficiently on a keyboard instrument so that it happens automatically whenever we put the fingers on the instrument,
- how to produce the best sound on the instrument so that it happens automatically and we don't have to relearn how to do it every time we learn a new piece,
- how to play stepwise or arpeggiated notes absolutely smoothly or like little drops of rain in any piece we're playing without ever having to consciously think about it,
- how to play a note whose intonation is exactly correct so naturally and so consistently that it just seems to happen every time we play it,
- where the strings that you have to play on your instrument are, so that you never have to look for them when you are playing,
- how to switch from one string to another, or one key to another, without ever having to think about it,
- how to switch from one valve to another effortlessly so that it all sounds like one note that just melds into another,
- when, how, and where you have to lift the palate to get to the next note or how to switch from chest voice to head voice in order to produce a singing voice that is seamless (this is called *passaggio*),
- how much air you need to play a section on one breath so that the body does it without thinking,
- whether it's best to play the passage with a different kind of breathing technique,
- where you have to stretch the arm because the slide on the instrument has to go a little farther than your arm reaches easily,
- how to improve flexibility so that we can get from one place to another on our instrument easily, and, finally, SACs
- aid the development of speed, evenness, and control in the playing of the instrument (or singing).

Think about a gymnast on the four-inch-wide bar who can balance perfectly while doing gymnastic moves that seem almost impossible to execute; that's exactly what SACs do for music students.

When we realize that the above list names just a few of the many things that the SACs teach us to do automatically, it is easy to understand how much time, how many years, musicians save in practice time just from devoting themselves to playing the SACs well.

Of course the trick is to be able to play the SACs completely accurately and automatically. Struggling through them laboriously isn't going to be helpful. They become valuable only after the student can play them absolutely perfectly without thinking about it, because that's when the technique transfers to whatever piece the student is learning.

SACs Are Models

Keep in mind that SACs are models of music. They are like model homes or form letters—examples of what someone's home or someone's letter can look like. Model homes are always clean because no one lives in them to mess them up, just as no one will find a grammatical error in form letters (hopefully). No one has to change sheets in a model home, because no one ever sleeps in the beds. In form letters no one has to worry about the grammar, because whoever originally wrote the form letter already made sure that the grammar was correct when the letter was composed. In both cases the models are perfect. However, they are not as complete as they are. They are meant to be examples, forms that we can use by filling in the blanks. They require the details that human beings put into them to make them reflect the personalities of the people who use them.

Similarly, scales, arpeggios, and chords are models, examples, patterns—the form letters of music, if you will. In and of themselves, they are not complete pieces of music. But when we incorporate those patterns into compositions that are written by great composers—well, that's when they become music. Until then they are mere patterns—musical form letters.

SACs Must Be Perfect

Unlike real music, the SACs don't have to be beautiful. Musicians don't have to think about whether to play them softly or loudly, whether to crescendo or diminuendo, or whether to play gently or passionately. They just have to play them technically completely accurately, in terms of notes and fingering, and totally uniform in touch, volume, and sound from beginning to end. The SACs, because they are models, can be perfect. And because they *can* be perfect, we must practice them until they *are* perfect.

And the strangest thing is this: when a musician can play the scales, arpeggios, and chords with that kind of accuracy, precision, uniformity, and perfection, the SACs actually are beautiful, rewarding, and exciting to the listener.

What no one realizes is that if a student conscientiously practices scales fifteen or twenty minutes a day every day as part of his regular routine, in a year or two that student will reach a level of technique that would otherwise have taken four or five years to attain. And that doesn't include the amount of time saved by not having to practice parts of music that are in those patterns. Isn't that reward enough to make the work worthwhile?

FOR PARENTS

Parents generally have no idea of the purpose or the value of the scales, arpeggios, and chords and therefore don't try to encourage their children to practice them.

But for young students SAC practice is vital. It develops the young muscles and the strength and stamina to play pieces of great length without fatigue. Many parents who help their children practice find that the little ones just refuse to practice SACs. Without SAC practice, though, the whole process of learning takes infinitely longer, and, what's worse, practicing the SACs the wrong way can be detrimental to the progress of the young student.

Oh, youngsters like playing SACs if they can do them fast. To children speed makes playing the SACs (or anything) *fun*. To young students accuracy and evenness aren't necessarily important, and that's what eventually gets them into big musical trouble.

Accuracy, Evenness, Uniformity

In order to make use of the SACs, the first rule is that they must be played absolutely accurately, uniformly, and completely evenly. From the moment the student starts the scale or the arpeggio until the last note, every note must have the same touch, the same intensity, the same loudness, the same speed, the same articulation, and the same anything else you can think of. From one end of the scale to the other, every note must be played the same way as the note that came before it and the one that will come after it. Therefore, SACs must be practiced slowly—really, really slowly—until they can be played absolutely correctly.

No Stopping and Starting

Young students hesitate or stop and start a lot while they are playing SACs because they play them fast (or faster than they should) long before they are capable of playing them correctly. Because the speed is too fast when they start, along the way they suddenly get stuck and have to stop. Maybe they have to think of where the next note is or what finger to use or whether or not to breathe in order to play the note. In any event, the fingers suddenly begin to hesitate until they can figure out how to get past the stuck part, and then they play fast again. That kind of playing teaches the hands how to play the notes unevenly and un-uniformly.

Since what is learned in the SACs very quickly transfers to how we play in real pieces, it's just a hop, skip, and a jump from playing SACs unevenly or inaccurately to playing pieces the same way. The chances are that a child who plays the SACs with the wrong fingering or wrong notes or who stops and starts along the way will also play the piece that way and never realize that it's wrong because he is so used to hearing the unevenness and hesitation.

A Parent's Job

Parents have a hard job here—encouraging the child to practice the SACs but also making sure that the child plays them very slowly, insuring that at the very least, the notes, fingering, volume, and intonation are absolutely correct. What might seem slow to the child (or even to the parent) isn't necessarily as slow as the SACs ought to be played. The parent should make sure the playing is e-x-t-r-e-m-e-l-y a-n-d p-a-i-n-f-u-l-l-y s-l-o-w and that the child watches every note he plays and that there is no stopping, starting, or hesitation along the way.

Make SAC Practice a Game

Here's an idea: Make a game of SAC practice. Get a costume police hat. Wear it when the child practices the SACs. If the child plays the scales too rapidly, write him a speeding ticket. On the other hand, if he plays them really slowly, write a commendation. Or give the *child* the police hat. Ask him to be the cop and monitor his own playing.

In any event, parents and all those who help the student practice should do their best to encourage practice of the SACs. It is really worth the effort.

FOR STUDENTS

Everyone—especially students—hates practicing the SACs. They complain that they are tedious and uninteresting. Students don't see the forest for the trees. They want to hear pieces. "Where's the music?" they say.

SACs Are Not Warm-Ups

When students finally agree grudgingly to practice scales, they use them for warm-ups. If you want to warm up, use a sweater. Use two sweaters. SACs aren't warm-ups. They are vital to technical proficiency.

Choose SACs

Okay, so it goes like this. Agreed, SACs are boring and, at the very least, uninteresting. Practice them anyway. The fact is that because they are so valuable it is more important to practice the SACs than pieces. Therefore, if you have a problem of time and must make a choice between practicing pieces and practicing SACs, choose the SACs. It will ultimately get you much further, and your technique will improve much faster.

Each Instrument Is Different

What I have said about SACs in this chapter has been very general and is meant for all music students. Of course for each instrument the practice of SACs must, by necessity, be a little different, since each instrument has its own peculiarities and limitations. For instance, a singer can only sing two, maybe three, octaves of scales, and he certainly can't sing chords. A clarinetist can only play scales one note at a time in perhaps three octaves, but pianists can play four octaves of scales, hands together.

A Few General Rules about SAC Practice

Practice scales and arpeggios over the greatest number of notes possible on your instrument, not just the notes where the instrument sounds the best. One of the purposes of learning scales, arpeggios, and chords is to increase the amount of notes the student is able to play or sing well. If students only play or sing scales within their comfort zone, the improvement will be less than if the student always tries to expand the notes he is capable of playing (or singing).

Wherever possible, practice scales and arpeggios in both directions, up and down. Actually, pianists and other keyboardists play sideways, but the sound goes up and down. Have you ever wondered if keyboard instruments should be set on their side? That way *up* would be *up*, and *down* would be *down*, and everyone would be much less confused.

Anyway, students sometimes think that playing the scale or arpeggio in one particular direction (either ascending or descending) is easier than going the opposite way. They therefore practice the easier direction and either postpone or altogether forget about going the other way. This actually does more harm than good. To keep the level of proficiency and improvement even, both directions should be practiced equally.

Always try to make the intonation and touch as correct and beautiful as possible. Pretend that you are on a stage, performing in front of a multitude of people, and that the SACs you are practicing are one of the great musical masterpieces of the century. Try to create the sound that you would like your audience to hear.

Don't try to practice the SACs fast. Don't worry. As you become more proficient, they will get faster by themselves. Do your best to make sure the elements—intonation, notes, fingering, and touch—are correct.

Keyboard players should always practice both hands together. No matter how tempting it is, never practice one hand alone. One of the most important purposes of SAC practice for keyboardists is developing the coordination of both hands that must do different things at the same time. Playing only one hand at a time defeats that purpose. Oh, and never play scales with the pedal. Pedal tends to mask the sound. In the practice of SACs we strive for precision, purity, and perfection. Special adornments spoil that effect.

Incidentally, guitarists really play scales in a strange way—they start on the first note of the scale but don't always end on the same note. Hmm, could that be because they have poor memories and forget the note from which they started by the time they get to the top?

How Many Fingers Do *You* Have?

Speaking of differences among instruments, you probably know that if you ask pianists and harpists how many fingers they have, they'll tell you "Ten fingers—five on each hand." That makes sense, right? However, did you know that string players say they have a thumb and four fingers on each hand? For string players their first finger is the index finger. (Yet if you ask the same string players how many toes they have, they say they have ten toes, five on each foot.) Hmm. How can they have ten toes but only eight fingers? Very strange. Likewise, clarinet players say they have eight fingers and two thumbs. They don't usually think of the thumb as a finger, because it generally isn't used to play, only to hold the instrument. That's just a bit of trivia you'll probably never use again, but I thought I'd throw it in.

Some Final Words

The next chapter refers particularly to piano. Therefore if you are one of those folks not studying piano, then feel free to skip it. But as a musician whose principal instrument is piano, I would have been hard put not to include it in this book.

Some folks feel that piano is more difficult because we play so many more notes than other musicians. Having learned several instruments in my lifetime, I can tell you from personal experience that piano is actually easier than any other instrument. With most other instruments the student must *create* the sound. If the string player doesn't put his finger in the correct place on the fingerboard, the note will be wrong or will sound like cater-wauling. If the wind player doesn't control his mouth correctly and breathe correctly the note will be wrong or sound like a bull moose in pain. The trombone player who doesn't put the slide in exactly the right position will play a wrong note, or the note won't sound altogether. There are no black and white keys to tell them where to play. For pianists the sounds are fixed. We can see where the notes are; we don't have to wiggle our fingers around to find them or figure out how to blow or breathe to play them. If we play the right keys, the notes will be the ones we want them to be. That's a big plus when learning an instrument.

Oh, and one last word. For many years folks have wondered whether to call us *pee-AN-ists* (with the accent on the *an*) or *PEE-an-ists* (with the accent on the *pee*). I vote for the former. Instrumentalists who play violins are called vi-o-LIN-ists; those who play flutes are called FLUTE-ists; those who play organ are OR-gan-ists. Therefore, we should be pee-AN-ists. Besides, putting the accent on the first syllable, as in PEE-an-ists, gives the whole profession a connotation that . . . well, we won't go into that. Just remember this: if any one asks you which pronunciation is correct, say pee-AN-ists. Tell them I said so, and I'm the teacher!

FOR INSTRUCTORS

Scales, arpeggios, and chords play a huge role in music. As instructors we all know that. However, getting *students* to recognize the importance of SAC practice is one of the great challenges of teaching music. It is surpassed only by the challenge of trying to get students to actually practice them. When students don't have much time, the first thing they skip is the SACs. "I can only practice a little while today. I'd rather spend the time on my pieces," they say.

It is very important that instructors discuss with their students the reasons that SACs are so important. Oh, I know, we all tell them, "Make sure you practice the scales, arpeggios, and chords. They are very important." But the truth is that we often let it go at that and don't tell them *why* they are very important. If students don't see the value in practicing something, they're not going to want to do it, especially if that something is repetitious and boring. Knowing exactly why scale, arpeggio, and chord practice is so crucial can make the difference between whether a student practices the SACs or not.

That same situation often happens with learning theory—the grammar of music, if you will. To a student who doesn't understand the connection between the theoretical concepts and their application in playing an instrument or singing, the study of theory is abstract and uninteresting. However, once the student makes that connection between the two, he suddenly feels that studying theory is like opening a door to a whole new world. Suddenly out of nowhere a student will say, "Oh, wow, I just noticed that this whole piece is filled with seconds and thirds," or "I just realized this whole section is just an extension of the musical idea that came before it," as if it's the revelation of a lifetime.

The same idea goes for helping students to want to practice SACs. (That's a bit of an oxymoron, isn't it? Sort of like wanting to do dishes. But you understand the concept, I'm sure.) Take the time to completely explain the purpose and value of learning SACs. Use some of the ideas in this chapter to help the students understand their importance.

Take some time during the lesson to show the student how much of the music contains patterns of scales, arpeggios, and chords. Give him a significant piece of music (a sonata, a symphony, something with several pages) to look at, and ask the student to point out the patterns of SACs, in order to help him realize that they are not just abstract exercises but are used all the time in music.

Be as demanding in the quality of a student's SAC practice as you are in the performance of his pieces. Require that the student's hand, arm, and body position be as correct as possible. Require that the production of the tone, the precision of the touch, and the uniformity of the playing be the same in every scale, all the time.

And last, please don't tell the students that SACs are just warm-ups. (Whenever I hear that, I always want to get the student a coat or a jacket.) While we may sometimes use long-note practice as a warm-up, the study of scales, arpeggios, and chords has nothing to do with weather, temperature, or warming up. Scales, arpeggios, and chords are critical to music, and learning how to play or sing them well benefits a student more than he can possibly imagine.

14

MOLTO APPASSIONATO

Don't Shoot the Piano Player

No other acoustic instrument can match the piano's expressive voice.

—Kenner Miller, musician

PRELUDE

"What instrument would you like to study, Jeffrey?" asked the teacher.

"Piano. I want to study piano," said Jeffrey in a very definite tone of voice.

The teacher smiled. "Why the piano?"

"This is why. Listen to the sounds it can make," Jeffrey answered. He put his hand on the bottom of the piano and played some notes. "Down here it sounds just like a tiger. Listen."

"Yes, I can hear it," the teacher responded.

"And up here it sounds like a chirping bird." He played some notes all the way up at the top of the piano.

Again, the teacher smiled and replied, "Yes, it certainly does."

The boy ran around to the side of the piano and reached inside the instrument, pulling his fingers along the strings. With his head almost inside the piano, he squealed, "And listen to how beautiful that sound is."

"Umm, yes, it's very . . ." began the teacher but Jeffrey was already back at the keys, playing more notes. He created loud sounds all over the piano and held his foot down on the pedal.

"Is that cool or what? No other instrument sounds like that."

Before the instructor could answer him, Jeffrey climbed under the piano and began to hit the bottom of the soundboard with his fists, gently—first slowly, then faster and faster. It sounded like a drum.

"Did you know you can play anywhere on the piano, not just on the keys? It makes wonderful sounds however you play it. You can make it sound like a drum, you can make it sound like a harp, you can make it sound like a bird, or a tiger. You can play happy music on it and sad music, and you can make it scary or friendly. The piano can sound like the whole orchestra, all rolled into one. I gotta learn to play this thing. I just love it. It makes me feel so good."

FOR EVERYONE

This chapter contains a great deal of detailed information for piano students because, as I said at the end of chapter 13, I am, after all, a pianist and have been for all of my life. Except where I talk about something particular for parents of young children, most of the data refers to all students, regardless of age. Therefore, parents, if your child is learning piano, please read this whole chapter carefully.

FOR PARENTS

- Think particularly about using an adjustable bench for your growing piano student. As the child grows, the seat can be made lower.
- A child or a short person studying piano will often need a box on which to put his feet so that they don't dangle. Make sure that the bottoms of both feet are sitting firmly on the top of the box.
- Children also can sit on phone books to raise themselves up.
- Never allow a child to play in flip-flops at the piano. They flip and flop while the child is playing and cause a major distraction to the student.
- Remember to white out all English letters, all finger numbers, and all lyrics in music for elementary students and to never put letters on the piano keys. Parents often feel sorry for young children when they are just starting piano and think that writing the English letters on the

instrument or in the music will help them. Actually, it does just the opposite, because it focuses their attention on the letters (with which they are familiar) instead of on the notes.

- In the beginning the child should play loudly, with a sure tone. Playing that way allows the ear to hear the note and the finger to feel it.

- Where young children are advanced enough to play octaves or big chords but their hands are not large enough to stretch, it is often wise to eliminate some of the notes to make the stretch easier.

- Help the child to find out what is the same and what is different in music during practice. If you point out the sameness or differences by noting that "Both these places have C and G in the left hand—let's try it," and then have the child just play that part a few times, before long the child will be able to play the part easily.

- Encourage the student to keep his eyes on the music at all times. Don't memorize first. Music at the beginning or intermediate level is not so difficult that it requires prior memorization before being able to practice it.

- Piano students need more encouragement than other students. While most other students can play in ensembles even at the elementary level, pianists don't generally become a part of groups until they are more advanced. They can't be accompanists because they aren't sufficiently proficient yet; they certainly can't be soloists yet; and they can't join a band because they play too many solo notes. So when they ask for company while practicing or an audience when they have learned something, or if they seem to need encouragement when they become frustrated, it's up to you to provide the encouragement enthusiastically.

- Young students sometimes practice scales and arpeggios in only one octave or in separate hands in the beginning. It is much better to start out practicing at least two octave scales in order to learn the thumb turns immediately. Although it is a little more difficult at the outset, within a short while it actually makes the learning easier.

- Young students want to play SACs fast. They don't care very much about accuracy and uniformity. SACs played wrong are *wrong* no matter how many times the student plays them. Remember that SAC practice is a habit. As the student gets accustomed to playing them, the SACs will automatically get faster. Once the SACs become fast, it will be very difficult to correct them. Therefore, it is imperative to make sure they are correct before they get fast.

FOR STUDENTS

Pianists don't hold their instruments in their hands, like violinists do, or cradle them in their arms, like guitarists, or hold them between their knees, like cellists, and they don't generally blow into them, like wind players. They sit in front of the instrument and touch the keys with their fingers. Therefore, the position of the body when they sit down to play is particularly important. Pianists must think about the kind of seat they use, how far away they are from the piano, how high up they are on the seat, and where their feet go. All musicians must think about these things, but especially pianists because they sit in front of the instrument to play it.

Sitting at the Piano

Here are a few rules about sitting at the piano. I've mentioned some of them before, but for pianists they are particularly important, and so I mention them again.

- Sit on an armless chair or a bench, preferably one that is adjustable.
- If you must stretch to reach the keys, you're too far way from the instrument, but don't sit so close that you feel squashed. Your upper arms should be at a ninety-degree angle to the keys, and your elbows should be at the same height as the keys. If your elbows are higher than the keyboard, you are sitting too high. If your elbows are lower than the keys, you're too low. Don't sit on throw pillows or pillows from your bed; they're too soft, and your body will sink into them. (Now you understand why I said to get an adjustable bench.)
- Taller students will need to sit farther away from the piano and lower than shorter students. Similarly, heavier students should sit farther away from the piano also.
- Your elbows should always be just a little bit forward of your body. If your elbows touch your sides, you are too close.
- Sit closer to the front of the chair, and keep your feet planted firmly on the floor. (Keeping your feet planted firmly on the ground is probably a good idea for anything you do.)

Hand Position

- With your fingers on the keys, hold your hand up so that your knuckles and wrist are high up and more or less level with each other.
- With your hand in that position, point the thumb and the pinky straight down toward the keys. They should look like columns holding up each side of your hand. Fold the other three fingers down so that the tips of the fingers just touch the keys. Point the fingers directly down toward the keys, from the knuckles (which meet the palm). The tips of the fingers should be directly under the knuckles of the palm, not pushed out.
- Your elbow should be about two inches below the wrist and level with the keys.
- Keep the hand firm but relaxed. There should be no tension anywhere.

That's the perfect hand position. Sometimes we must stretch out the hand when playing big chords, but even then we contract the fingers when the chords are finished.

What Not to Do with Your Hands

- Don't point your fingers out in front of your hand. If you can see your nails, you are playing incorrectly.
- Don't curve your fingers so that the hand looks like a claw. If your knuckles are depressed, the position is wrong. (You might talk to a psychiatrist about their depression.)
- Don't stretch your fingers flat out in front of your hands. Playing with flat fingers is like trying to run with skis on your feet. Even if the finger tips are curved, if they are two inches out past the knuckle, the position is wrong.
- Never play on the side of the thumb or the flat of the pinky. The pinky and thumb should never lay flat on the keys. The tips of the pinky and thumb should hit the keys.

Learning the Notes on the Keyboard

Learning the notes on the keyboard is particularly easy for piano students. The letters are the white keys. The black keys are like little landmarks that indicate where the white keys are. There are only seven letters in the musical alphabet, A, B, C, D, E, F, and G. They are repeated seven times in order from the left to the right of the keyboard (ABCDEFG, ABCDEFG, ABCDEFG, and so on.) When you play the letters forward from left to right—ABCDEFG—the pitch (not volume) goes up; when you play them backward from right to left—GFEDCBA—the pitch goes down.

Below are the lyrics to a song I wrote called "C Is on the Left of the Two Black Keys," which teaches the letters and their placement on the keyboard. You can either say it or sing it. (The song can be found on the CD accompanying *The Husky Gang Teaches Piano Song and Story Book*, published by Warner Brothers.) Do this rhythmically five minutes in the morning and five minutes at night every day for two weeks.

C is on the left of the two black keys; [the first white note just to the left of the group of two black keys is C]
E is on the right of the two black keys;
D is in the middle of the two black keys;
F is on the left of the three black keys; [think that there's an *F* in the word *left*]
B is on the right of the three black keys; [you want to be *right*, not wrong]
Where is A? A is on the left of B. where is G? G is on the right of F.

Sit at the piano when saying this exercise. Find the white key that is on the left of the two black keys anywhere on the piano, and play it. That's a C. It doesn't matter which C you play. Just make sure you are playing C and not another letter.

Students learn music notation through a combination of several exercises:

- saying where the note is and then playing it in its correct place on the keyboard (which leads to simply recognizing the notes, like someone who eventually sees that c-a-t spells *cat* and does not have to sound out each letter),
- watching the direction of the notes (whether they move up or down, stepwise or by skips),
- knowing the hand staff, and
- being able to play without looking at the keyboard.

This is a good time to look back to chapter 7 to review my five-pronged approach to helping students learn notation. Remember that the five prongs were flashcards, hand staff, note recognition, direction of the notes, and, especially, eyes front, heads up.

Flashcards

The flashcards suggested in chapter 7 are 5" × 7", and they cover four octaves of notes on the piano. On the front side of the card are a staff, a clef sign, and a note. On the back are both the answer and a diagram of the keyboard, showing the placement of the note. Remember the buddy system—one person holds each card with the note facing the student and the answer facing the holder. The buddy looks at the answer, and the student must say the note and play it in its proper place.

Before starting to use flash cards: Draw a line for middle C below the treble clef staff or above the bass clef staff with an arrow going up or down from there to the printed note to show the direction and distance of the note from the middle C line. Using the right hand if the note is in the treble clef and the left hand if the note is in the bass clef, the student should put a finger on middle C and

- identify the clef sign (e.g., treble clef or bass clef),
- identify the placement of the note (e.g., space four),
- identify the letter name of the note (e.g., E), and

- slide the finger up or down from middle C to the note on the flashcard and play that note.

Place a pencil on the keyboard at bass clef line one G, another pencil on treble clef line five F, and a third pencil on middle C to indicate the boundaries of the complete staff. Remember to gradually reduce the card size while speeding up the response time.

Knowing where C is on the keyboard only tells part of the story. The left of the two black keys tells "where *all* the Cs live." You might call that a house number; it doesn't tell "what street" each C lives on. Every note on the keyboard not only has a name but also occupies a particular line or space and clef sign on the staff. Therefore, each flash card note has not only a "house number" but also a "street name."

Hand Staff

The section in chapter 7 that refers to the hand staff is briefly summarized here.

Hold your hand in front of your face so that the back of your hand faces you and the fingers are perpendicular to your body; the thumb is the lowest and the pinky the highest finger. Spread out the fingers so that the fingers and the spaces between them look like the lines and spaces of the staff.

The fingers represent the lines of the staff, and the spaces between the fingers represent the spaces between the lines. The thumb is line one (the lowest line of the staff), and the pinky is line five (the highest line). Space one, the lowest space (between lines one and two), will be between your thumb and index finger. Space four, the highest space, will be between fingers four and five. The right hand is the treble clef, the left hand the bass clef. In that position say:

- the lines of the treble clef are E, G, B, D, F, EGBDF, EGBDF (holding the right hand up, wiggling each finger in turn as you say it, making many repetitions);
- the lines of the bass clef are G, B, D, F, A, GBDFA, GBDFA (as above);
- the spaces of the treble clef are F, A, C, E (pointing to the spaces between the right-hand fingers, repeating, as above); and
- the spaces of the bass clef are A, C, E, G (pointing to the spaces between the left-hand fingers, and repeating, as above).

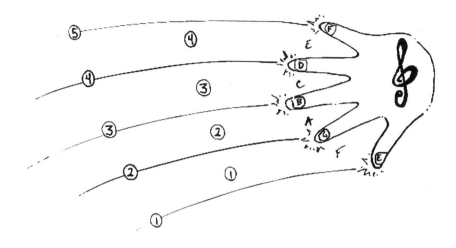

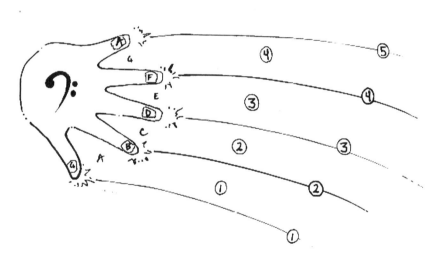

Always say the lines and spaces of each clef the same way. Make many repetitions of each sentence, increasing the speed of the sentence until you are saying it in one breath. Point with the other hand to each line (finger) or space as you say them. Do this exercise twice a day, five minutes in the morning and five minutes at night. Whenever you say the lines or spaces of the staff, always say them from the bottom (line one) up to the top (line five) or from the bottom space up to the top.

Note Recognition and Direction of Notes

Again, look back at chapter 7.

Eyes Front, Heads Up

Piano students particularly need to work on watching the music instead of their hands. Students of other instruments do this naturally, because they can't see the notes they are playing on their instruments. However, because the keyboard is right in front of the pianist, the impulse to look down at the keys is almost irresistible. Force yourself to look at the music and learn where the keys are by sound and touch. When you play by touch, mistakes help the fingers learn. It is actually better to allow the fingers to hit the wrong notes or play in the cracks. As you play the note, listen to determine if it is correct. If not, look down to see how far you are from the note you want to hit. Then play it again, adjusting the distance. After a few tries, you'll hit the correct note. Of course, always look down to find the first note on the keyboard when you begin a piece.

Try this: Hit a white key in the center of the piano while looking at it. Jump up about one octave and hit another white key with the same hand while looking at it. Look at the first note, and hit it again. Jump to the second note, and hit it again, still looking. Hit the first note again, and then jump to the second, this time *without* looking. Your hand will probably hit a note very close to the one you were aiming for. After a few tries you will be able to jump from the first note to the second without looking at all. This is the way pianists learn to make huge leaps without having to look at the keys.

Down to the Bottom of the Key

When you hit the key, make sure the note goes all the way down to the bottom. Many beginning piano students play with a very tentative touch. Instead of hitting the keys solidly, they drag their fingers around onto the piano keys and push them down. Because sometimes the keys go down and sometimes they don't the fingers feel as if they are walking on a slippery surface where they can fall at any moment. Their fingers are unsteady and unsure, just like the legs of beginning ice skaters. Because beginning skaters are afraid that they will fall, they never lift their feet off the ice; they just shuffle them around. In order to skate, the legs must be able to work independently of each other. Skaters must learn to lift their feet off the ice, one at a time, balance themselves on their feet, and shift the weight from one foot to another. Pianists must do exactly the same with their fingers. Playing with a solid tone means hitting each key decisively, down to the bottom. Language arts teachers tell students not to mumble and to enunciate each word carefully. They aren't telling them to scream. It's the same thing with playing the piano.

Try this: Lift the index finger about 1½ inches above the note you want to play. Using only the strength of the finger, in one fluid motion hit the key quickly all the way down to the bottom. This develops strength in the fingers and gives a solid tone and a uniform sound to the music you play. Starting the movement from above the key creates the same kind of thrust that a golfer generates when he pulls the club back before hitting the ball or that the pitcher produces when he throws the ball from behind his shoulder. It gives more impetus to the movement. You can even practice this on a tabletop. Remember this: play down to the bottom of each key; no timid mouse music.

Tight Muscles

If your hands hurt when you are practicing, look for tight muscles in your arms or hands. Watch out especially for the thumb and the wrist. If the thumb is relaxed, usually the rest of the arm will also be relaxed. Sometimes students inadvertently tighten their wrists as they play. The arm becomes like a steel rod from the finger knuckles to the elbow. After a while, the student gets accustomed to playing with a tight arm. If you notice that any part of your arm becomes tense or locked in place, stop playing immediately, and consciously shake out your hands.

Economy of Motion

Move your arms and fingers as little as possible when you play. Don't make any excess motion. Move the fingers exactly where they need to go, in exactly the time it takes to get there. When making a jump, lift your hand slowly enough that when you bring it down onto the key it must play it will be exactly at the correct moment, not early and not late. Think *economy of motion*.

Whenever you must push a thumb under, make a wrist turn, or change the position of the hand, don't hesitate. If you make the movement quickly, the hand will learn to make position changes instantaneously. If you make the hand movements slowly or hesitantly, the arm, wrist, or fingers will always lag behind, and you won't be able to speed them up later when you want to play faster. However, always remember to straighten out the hand immediately after a thumb turn or change of position.

When you have to hit a key that is a little distant from where you have been playing, stretch the hand out as close as possible to where it has to go, and lead with the finger you're going to play with next. This will create a smaller jump.

When you jump from one place to another on the keyboard, try to move horizontally in the air to the next place. Don't let the whole arm go up high and then across. Instead move the arm in a low arc so that most of the motion will be horizontal.

Women's and children's hands are usually smaller than men's, and they sometimes have trouble playing big chords and octave passages. To play pieces with large stretches, both the palm and the fingers must be well stretched and flexible. There are many stretching exercises that develop elasticity and flexibility in the fingers.

Developing Independence of the Hands

To develop independence in the hands, practice playing one hand alone, and play the other hand in the air, in your lap, or on the wood of the instrument, instead of on the keys. Or play one hand alone and imagine the other. When a passage is difficult it sometimes helps to practice one hand at a time in order to find out what's happening in that hand. You might notice, "Oh, that's just a little arpeggio repeated for the whole line." Of course, you *might* find that "Wow, that part will need a lot of work." That's good, too.

Analyze the Music

Pianists must especially analyze the printed page in order to know what's coming in the music. We play a lot of notes, and it is difficult to think about all of them at the same time, not to mention all the other things we have to keep in mind. If we can find recognizable patterns of SACs and phrases that repeat themselves with small variations, the piece will be much easier to learn. Remember that most other instrumentalists are reading only one line of music and one clef at a time. We must play two clefs and two staves at the same time. We need all the help we can get.

Rhythm

Always count louder than you play so that you hear the counts as if someone else were calling them out to you. Remember that counting out loud shows you exactly where the counts go and which notes to put on those counts.

Piano students get so involved in playing the notes that they sometimes simply forget to count. A student sometimes starts out counting and playing, but, as the piece progresses or as the student becomes less sure of the music, the counting gets softer and softer, and eventually there is silence. If a student understands the rhythm and can count the beats with confidence, he can play anything. Piano students can count out loud easier than other students, because they are not doing anything else with their mouth while they are playing. Because they can count out loud, they should. Listen, the mouth isn't doing anything. Give it a job. Make it count—out loud.

Write the Counts between the Staves

Write in the counts in the space between the treble clef and the bass clef. If you write them in that space, you can see them as you play the music. Don't forget to write where the *and* goes. Then just say what you wrote. Try it! It's easy.

SAC Practice

In addition to what I have already said about SACs, below are some SAC rules especially for piano students. Although some piano students practice SACs in contrary motion, most learn them first in *similar motion* (both hands going in the same direction at the same time). The information below refers to learning the SACs in similar motion.

Remember how I spoke earlier about hitting the piano key down to the bottom? SACs are the perfect place to practice the attack of the finger on the key. (Sometimes I wonder about the language of pianists. We speak of *hitting* the key when we refer to playing a note and the *attack* of the finger, which means how we make the key go down, quickly or slowly. Makes us sound violent, doesn't it? Language is very confusing, but then, violinists *draw* their bows across their instruments, and clarinetists *triple tongue* notes. So, I guess the oddity all evens out in the end.) The SACs help students develop the tactile sense of playing the notes on the piano.

When you play the SACs be watchful of the following:

- Play all SACs with high palms and knuckles. Play on the tips of the fingers just behind the nails. (That's why we keep the nails short.)
- Use the pinky and the thumb as columns to keep the rest of the hand up.

- The knuckles of the fingers where the fingers meet the palms should always be showing. If the knuckles are depressed, you are playing incorrectly.
- Make sure you cannot see your fingernails when you are playing.
- The thumb should tuck under the hand immediately after you play it. If you are playing a C Major scale, as you play the second finger of the right hand on the D, the thumb should tuck under and push under the fingers to the right as much as possible, exiting only *after* the E, to play the F. After the F, when the second finger plays the G, the thumb tucks under again and exits only to play the C at the eighth note of the scale.
- Don't slide the finger on the piano key. Sometimes in a thumb crossing a student will play the third or fourth finger farther out and then slide the finger on the key toward the other fingers. The place where you slide the finger *to* is where it belongs in the first place. Don't put it someplace else first and then slide to where it should be.
- When you are at the lowest point of the scale, the left arm should be straight from elbow to the fingers, and the right arm should be bent from the elbow to the fingers. Similarly, when you are at the highest point of the scale, the right arm should be straight from elbow to the fingers, and the left arm should be bent.
- Never stretch out the arm to the side or move on the bench as you go up or down the scale to get closer to the keys you are playing. Lean over onto one haunch to play the lowest or the highest notes. That immediately brings the hands into the correct position, where one arm is bent and the other is straight. While the body leans to one side, position your head so that your nose is in the center between your two hands (above the keyboard, not on it). Slowly straighten out the body as you play closer to the center of the piano, and as you move to the other end of the keyboard slowly shift the weight to the other haunch.
- Regardless of where we play on the instrument—down, up, or middle—the touch (how high we lift each finger to hit the note), finger placement (where we put our fingers), volume, and speed must be uniform on every note, and both hands must hit each note of the scale, arpeggio, or chord at the same time.
- In each series of seven notes, the fourth finger in each hand only plays once, but the third finger plays twice.
- Say the key signature of the scale you are playing before you begin (e.g., D Major has two sharps, F♯ and C♯).
- Practice the SACs sufficiently slowly so that you don't have to stop to look for the notes or fingers while you are playing. The SACs should

be slow enough to allow you to think, correct any mistakes before they happen, and play without stopping or hesitation. The whole point of SAC practice is uniformity and evenness. If you have to stop, you are not playing evenly. Don't allow the scale to get faster until the fingering is absolutely correct, the hands play exactly together, and the touch is uniform. Once everything is correct, the hands will naturally adjust the speed as you become more proficient.

- Use the metronome to control the speed of the scale and the arpeggio.
- As you practice, if a finger is wrong, stop immediately. Don't just fix the mistake and go on.
- Never drop onto the side of the thumb or the flat of the pinky when you are playing a scale or arpeggio. This creates an up-down-up-down roll of the wrist that wastes motion and makes the sound uneven. The high thumb/pinky position stops that.
- Place the left hand so that it starts at the lowest note possible in that key, but don't go below the very lowest B. The right hand should be one octave above the left hand at all times if you are practicing the scale in similar motion.
- Practice the scales and arpeggios, going up and down. The highest note of the scale should not be repeated when beginning the descent. Similarly, if you go down and then up, the lowest note should not be repeated when you begin the ascent (e.g., up-down is FGAB CBAGF or FED CDEF is down-up).
- Always practice four octaves up and four octaves down (or at the very least two octaves), both hands together in both the scale and the arpeggio. Don't start by learning only one octave and then trying to add octaves later.
- Accent the first of every four notes in the scale and arpeggio. That puts a nice emphasis on the highest note and the lowest note. Although some people play the arpeggios in *triplets* (groups of three notes), if you accent the first of every four arpeggio notes you accent the highest note and the final bottom note, just as it does in the scales.
- The arpeggio should be half the speed of the scale, and the chords should be half the speed of the arpeggio. Play one arpeggio note to every two scale tones.
- Don't always practice SACs in an ascending and then descending pattern. Also practice them descending and then ascending. Students often learn the fingering going up easily but make mistakes on the way down because they forget the fingering. Reversing the direction in which you practice the SACs helps to memorize the descending fingering.

- When you practice the arpeggio after the scale, the last note of the scale *becomes* the first note of the arpeggio without repetition. As you hit the final note of the scale, stretch out the fingers into the arpeggio pattern and play the second note of the arpeggio without repeating the first.
- At our institute piano students play the scale first, then the arpeggio, and, last, the chord sequence. First, students learn to play the chord in root position only. Then they learn to play it in root position and two *inversions*. Inversions are varying positions in which you can play chord tones. There's more information about inversions in the glossary.
- When playing chords in different positions, change the fingers in the air. If you try to change them after you've moved to the new position, you'll hesitate.
- Keep the wrist level, and play each note without moving the wrist up or down so that the scale and arpeggio have a uniform and an even touch. Don't play a note in a scale with a lowered wrist and then after you have played it try to raise the wrist. This rolling hand motion creates an uneven sound.
- If you are playing a series of chords that are on different notes but in the same position, it is sometimes easier and more convenient to play the whole series with the *same* fingerings. In that case make the hand firm (not tight), and with an easy motion just keep changing notes, not fingers.
- Keep the fingers that you are not using in the chord out of the way, and hit all the notes you *are* playing exactly at the same time and with a sure tone.
- Spell the letters of the chord out loud each time before you play them. Say them in root position, regardless of the position in which you play them. The G-Major chord is spelled G B D, regardless of whether the G, the B, or the D is on the bottom.
- Never look at the keys when you spell the chord. Think of the letters first, and say them in root position. Then make your fingers play the notes you said. Do not look at your hands when you say the chords, and never play the chord first and then say the letters.

Keep in mind that playing the SACs forms the habits we carry over to playing everything else. Those habits can be either good or bad. As you become more proficient at playing them, the SACs automatically get faster. Therefore, it is imperative to make sure they are correct before they get fast.

Pedal Practice

Pianos have pedals. Look below the keyboard near the floor. See those little feet sticking out between the legs of the piano? Those are pedals. Some pianos have two pedals, some have three. The pedal on the extreme right—the damper pedal—is the one most often used. When you push it down, it makes every note you play continue to sound as long as the pedal is down. When you lift the pedal, the sound stops. Therefore, it is important to play the correct notes when using the damper pedal and to lift the pedal periodically to clear the sound. Otherwise no one will be able to hear individual notes, and the music will sound as mushy as oatmeal.

The pedal on the extreme left is the mute pedal. It makes the sound of all the notes softer and less percussive as long as the pedal stays down. The mute and the damper pedals can be played together by using both pedals simultaneously. When both pedals are pushed down at the same time, all the sounds accumulate but are softer and a little gentler. Of course, if you play the pedals but don't play any notes, nothing at all will sound.

The third pedal—the one in the middle (the sostenuto pedal)—holds only the first note or the first chord that you play. No matter how long you hold down that pedal, it holds only the first tone and doesn't pick up any other notes. It is used less often than the other two pedals.

I'm not going to say too much about the pedals for now, because beginning students don't usually use them. Instructors generally don't teach pedaling until piano students are more advanced. Students first need to be confident in their playing before the pedals are added. Therefore, the following information is just a heads up. It's always nice to know what's coming, even if it's not going to be here for a while.

- It's tricky to coordinate the hand and the foot at the same time, but you drive a car with both your hands and your feet, don't you? Athletes and children learn to jump rope coordinating their feet and their hands. You'll get used to it.
- Using the damper pedal is like adding sugar to a cake batter: too much and you'll spoil the cake, but not enough and it'll be too dry. Students need to know exactly how much pedal to use, and not a bit more. Otherwise overpedaling can ruin the piece.
- Young students usually learn the use of the pedal later than adult students (around the age of ten, eleven, or twelve, depending on the height of the student) because their feet are too short to reach the pedal. The good news is that a lot of piano music, especially at the early

levels, doesn't require pedal. Generally, by the time a student advances to the point where the music played requires pedal, the student's legs are usually long enough to reach them.

FOR INSTRUCTORS

The vast majority of music instructors teach piano (probably because there are more piano students than students of any other instrument). Most of them do a wonderful job. Some instructors, um, need a little help.

There are piano instructors who are an inspiration to us all. They know their subject backward and forward. Their enthusiasm bubbles over, their sense of creativity knows no bounds, and their love of teaching touches every student with whom they work. For them teaching piano isn't an occupation or even a career. It is one of the great joys of their lives. Coincidentally, those instructors always seem to have the very best students.

For others, teaching is just a job, tedious and without much emotional reward. For them, there is no joy in what they do. Before long their lackluster attitude rubs off on their students, who lose interest in their lessons. Piano teachers seem to suffer from this malaise much more than instructors of other instruments.

Sometimes all that is needed to transform a ho-hum piano teacher into an instructor that students remember forever are some fresh ideas, a little inspiration, and a way to get the creative juices flowing again. That's what I have tried to provide in this chapter.

It is certainly not my intention to tell piano instructors what to teach or even how to teach. However, I hope that some of the ideas in this section will help instructors realize that thinking a little beyond the textbook, a little beyond the required Standards, and perhaps a tad outside the box will not only inspire their students but also help regenerate the instructor's own creative ideas. With a little imagination, a lot of dedication, and a real love of teaching, every piano instructor can be that very special teacher forever remembered by their students.

⑮

CANTANDO E ESPRESSIVO

The Sweetest Song

When I sing, trouble can sit right on my shoulder and I don't even notice.

—Sarah Vaughn, singer

PRELUDE

"I have a most unusual situation, and I hope you can help me resolve it," the gentleman began.

"I'll certainly try," the voice instructor answered gently. "What's the problem?"

"Well, I am a minister at a church here in town. We have a very small choir, and I help them out by volunteering to sing with them because I'm the only tenor they have."

"That's very nice of you. So what's the problem?" the instructor asked.

The young man continued. "It's like this. There are choir rehearsals Monday and Thursday, and I also give two sermons a week, so I use my voice a lot. By Sunday evening, I have a sore throat almost every week. This just can't go on. The doctor has told me that I need to learn how to preserve my voice so I don't strain it so much. He said that if I don't, within a few years I could do permanent damage to my throat, and I might not have any voice left to preserve. He said I should talk with a good voice instructor, and he recommended you."

"Have you had a complete checkup to make sure there is nothing physiologically wrong with your throat?"

"Yes, the doctor says everything is fine except that my throat gets sore when I speak and when I sing. I have even taken to using a microphone for my sermons in order to stress my throat less. It helps, but I still develop a sore throat whenever I sing. Can you help me? I have heard that voice instructors can teach students how to preserve and protect the voice."

"Hmmm," said the teacher. "That's true, but first let's vocalize the voice and see what it sounds like so I know what I have to work with. Would you stand up, please?"

"Of course. Do you want me to sing a song or something?" asked the gentleman. "I'm sorry. I didn't bring any of my music."

"Oh, no, that's not necessary. I'm just going to play some little patterns of notes on the piano, and you're going to follow them with your voice. Here, let me show you." She sat down at the piano, and the young man stood by her side.

The teacher played five notes up and down the keyboard. "I just want you to sing that pattern on the syllable *ah* at the same time that I play it. We'll keep repeating the pattern, each time, a little bit higher, like this." She demonstrated on the piano. "Can you do that?"

"Yes, I guess so," he answered. "It certainly doesn't sound difficult."

They began the exercise. After a few repetitions, the teacher stopped. "You have a lovely voice. It's deep and rich. Does this make your throat hurt?"

He shook his head to indicate that it didn't. "No, it's very comfortable. It doesn't bother me at all," he replied.

"Good. Let's continue." She started the pattern again, and the young man immediately joined in. Little by little, the exercise got higher and higher. Suddenly, the instructor stopped. "No, no, not like that," she admonished. "Sing in your natural voice. Don't go into *falsetto*."

"What's falsetto?" the young man asked. He had never heard the term before.

The instructor answered quickly, "A man can allow his voice to slip into a very high range that's similar to where women sing. It's not a natural voice and requires forcing the larynx to do something it shouldn't be doing. That's called *falsetto*. For this exercise I only want to hear what your voice can do in its natural state."

"But I always sing up high with the choir. That's what they need. They need a high male voice," the man replied.

"Hmm. That's not your natural voice. Here, let's try the exercise again. I'll show you where your range ends."

The instructor began again on a lower note, and the young man followed with his voice. After several repetitions, each a little higher, she stopped him. "There. That's the end of where you should be singing. Watch—at the very next note, you were going to push the voice into another kind of singing that is not natural for your range. That forces the voice. You have a beautiful, rich, baritone sound. You're certainly not a tenor. You're not even close to being a tenor."

"Wow," he answered. "I almost never sing in that low range, even though it's very comfortable for me. The choir needs me to sing the high notes. Maybe that's why I've been getting these sore throats."

"That's certainly a good possibility. You also need to learn how to protect the voice so that you are not pushing so hard when you sing, but I think if you stop forcing your voice to sing such high notes your throat will hurt a lot less."

"You seem to have resolved my problem already," the gentleman marveled. "When can we start lessons?"

The instructor laughed. "How's next week?"

FOR EVERYONE

Everyone Likes to Sing

Everyone likes to sing. People sing in the shower. They sing in their cars along with CDs and the radio. They sing along with their favorite vocalists on TV. They buy karaoke machines and pretend they're a singing superstar. And of course everyone knows that birds sing. Even dogs sing. Well, they don't exactly sing, but . . . It seems like the whole world wants to sing. Unfortunately, most people haven't a clue about how to go about it.

Natural Isn't Enough

Lots of people think that because singing is such a "natural" thing to do, anyone can open their mouth and the voice that comes out will automatically be great. They have no idea what vocal training is; they think that taking voice lessons means that all they will have to do is learn songs. They don't realize that the voice is a musical instrument and that students who study singing must learn how to play their instrument just as they would if they were learning guitar, violin, oboe, piano, or trombone.

A Few Myths

Some people think that with a few months of lessons they'll be ready to make a CD or music video that will be number one on the charts for the next fifty years. And, of course, there are those who think that with proper instrumental backup and ear-splitting amplification a good voice is no longer necessary. Yes, I know; you've heard stories about singers with little or no vocal training who went from oblivion to the top of the charts "overnight." However, that's the exception to the rule, and such a giant jump often results in very short-lived fame, followed by years of negative effects that are unwanted, unwelcome, and sometimes permanent.

What Vocal Students Must Learn

In order to sing, students must first learn vocal technique—how to use the vocal apparatus in order to *create* a good sound and how to preserve that apparatus in order to be able to sing for many years to come.

The better and more permanent solution is to find the best vocal instructor possible and make sure that the student receives wonderful training in vocal technique from the ground up. That includes:

- learning how to breathe and how to use breath to support and control sound,
- understanding and developing the parts of the body that create and control sound,
- learning what the vocal apparatus is, how it works, and how to make it work the way it should in order to protect the voice,
- learning to place sound and syllables exactly where they should be, and
- ultimately developing the natural voice to the highest level that it can achieve.

In order to do all that, the student or the parent of the student must first do diligent research to find a really good instructor.

A Need for Caution

An inferior instructor can be dangerous for the student. Yes, I said dangerous, not just a waste of time and money or discouraging for the student . . . *dangerous*! The vocal apparatus is not like other instruments; if it breaks or gets ruined, you can't go out and buy another one; there's only one per customer. Unfortunately, improper vocal training can damage the voice, sometimes forever. Even if the damage isn't forever, it could take months or years to heal. Therefore, everything I said in the chapter on finding a good instructor is particularly important for a vocal student.

FOR PARENTS

Children Express Musicality by Singing

Some parents think their child should have voice lessons because he sings every song he hears on the radio or on TV. While that may, indeed, indicate an innately musical child for whom music lessons would be beneficial, it does not necessarily mean that child should have voice lessons.

Children express natural musicality by singing and moving their bodies in rhythmic response to sounds they hear, because they don't know any other way. Perhaps they've never heard another instrument, or they've never seen one, or there isn't one around for them to explore. It is better for such children to have music lessons on a pitched instrument, a piano or keyboard, violin, or guitar and develop strength, stamina, and fine motor skills first. Later the child can begin voice lessons after the vocal cords, diaphragm, lungs, and other parts of the body have sufficiently matured.

Premature Training Can Cause Permanent Damage

Premature vocal training can do serious damage to an immature body. Therefore, families should really be cautioned against giving young children between the ages of two and seven vocal lessons. Their muscles are just too fragile to support it. Learning vocal technique even for older children is dangerous unless the child is especially big in stature and stamina, with strong muscles, a naturally strong and vibrant voice, and a very pure sound. And, believe me, kids like that are few and far between.

Many parents don't realize that vocal lessons are not the same as merely singing songs. Vocal technique is strenuous exercise that taxes many muscles of the body, especially a child's muscles. Children's vocal cords are very fragile and easily damaged. Pushing, stretching, or forcing the throat muscles to produce sounds that are louder, higher, more intense, or in any way beyond the normal capacity or range of a child can be very detrimental to the child's physiological development and result in long-term damage.

Some parents want their young children to learn to sing songs so that they can put them into pageants or competitions that require contestants to have a specific talent. They think that learning to sing will take less time than learning other instruments and won't require the degree of training that "regular" music lessons do.

Invariably, the child learns to sing songs by belting them out—which often gets high marks from the judges and loud applause from the audience but does nothing to protect the voice from injury.

Learning Music Notation Is a Must

Vocal students, like everyone else, should learn to read music as soon as possible. As I said in the section on improvisation, not learning to read notation is not a viable option for a student of music. Learning only to play or only to sing is comparable to speaking a language without being able to read or write it. It's only part of the story. To achieve true music literacy, a student must be able to play his instrument (or sing) and read and write music as well. Students learn this most easily by playing a pitched instrument. Since vocalists eventually need to be able to accompany themselves anyway, learning to play either piano or guitar is not only warranted but necessary for a wanna-be singer.

Voice Change

Preteen and teenage students (particularly boys) should not have vocal lessons while their voices are changing. During that time the vocal apparatus is particularly fragile. Boys' voices change somewhere between the ages of twelve and fourteen, and as they go through puberty the vocal cords and other muscles thicken and strengthen. I have seen boys with angelic soprano voices leave for summer camp in late May and return in September as near baritones. What many people don't know is that girls' voices also change, but slower and less dramatically. A teenage boy's voice generally takes anywhere from four months to a year to change, while a girl's voice changes gradually over a period of several years, perhaps beginning around eleven and not ending until about fifteen. While it is less damaging for a girl to begin voice lessons during the change than for a boy (because the mutation is so gradual in a female), it is nevertheless preferable to wait until the mutation process is almost over before starting vocal instruction.

Other Options

I am not suggesting that youngsters or preteens should not sing songs. Not at all. However, there is a big difference between singing songs and learning vocal technique. Often, enrolling a child in a chorus satisfies his urge to sing and offers the added advantage of a peer-group environment. In most vocal ensembles the choral members meet a few times a week in rehearsal to learn songs. These meetings culminate in periodic performances throughout the year. Although such groups do begin their rehearsals with a few vocal exercises, the members of the group primarily learn to sing songs but not *how* to sing.

FOR STUDENTS

Different Strokes for Different Folks

There are many different styles of singing—pop, country, jazz, gospel, contemporary, classical, Broadway, opera, zarzuela, rock, rap, hip-hop, barbershop to name just a few. People can sing solo (alone) or in duets, quintets, choirs, and choruses. They might be accompanied by one person, a band, or a whole orchestra, or they might sing a cappella (without accompaniment). Each style puts different demands on the voice, and although there is some overlapping, most singers stick with only a couple of styles, and those styles are generally closely related. Regardless of what style of music a person chooses to learn to sing, the best way to proceed is to begin with vocal-technique training. Regardless of the age of the student, good vocal technique teaches:

- total breath control,
- well-enunciated diction,

- accurate intonation,
- appropriate dynamic presentation,
- the ability to connect melody lines,
- a thorough understanding of the text,
- the ability to communicate the thoughts and emotions of the music to the listener,
- the ability to project the words and music so that the listener hears them,
- cooperation between the singer and the band, orchestra, or accompanist,
- familiarity with the accompaniment as well as the melody line, and
- stage presence.

Other Things a Singer Should Know

In addition to vocal technique, singers should learn

- the use of the microphone or other amplification (how to hold or position a mic, when to use it or not),
- the differences in vocal production and projection when a microphone is used, and
- how to coordinate dancing, acting, and movement on the stage with the delivery of a song.

General Information

Here's some general information that anyone who wants voice training should know:

- Students of vocal technique (how to sing) will first sing many exercises before they learn a song. Through these exercises students actually learn how to build a voice and how to create sounds that are pleasing.
- Everyone can sing. Not everyone can sing beautifully. However, everyone can improve his natural voice to some degree, provided the voice is mature enough to sustain the rigors of vocal technique.
- There are certain kinds of voices that seem to be meant for one kind of singing or another. A voice may have a strong Broadway quality to it, or maybe a Nashville sound to it, or a very rich tone that might be best served in classical music or opera. Generally, when first exploring the student's voice the instructor can tell the quality of the voice, what

the range is (how high or low the person can sing), and what kind of music is best suited for that kind of voice.

- As a student gets older the voice generally drops somewhat in pitch. Singers (regardless of whether they are male or female) lose a few higher notes and gain a few lower ones as they age. In addition, the vibrato (the slight trembling sound that a voice has when singing) widens as a person gets older.

- Falsetto—the unnaturally high, shrill sound a man can generate when he sings way up high beyond his range—is not natural to the male singing voice. Tenors, those males with high voices, still sound like men when singing in their natural ranges. When a man sings in falsetto, however, he sounds more like a woman. Even if a man slips into falsetto easily, the falsetto voice is not a natural voice. Long ago boys who had beautiful soprano voices had surgery to prevent the voices from changing during puberty. When they grew up they retained their soprano voices. They were called castrati. (For those of you who are interested, the Internet has a lot of information about castrati, but I don't think very many doctors do that operation anymore, and I don't think too many families want their young sons to have the operation anyway.)

- In the beginning of learning vocal technique, it is better to sing songs in Italian, French, and Spanish, because the vowels are easier to pronounce, and the consonants are softer on the tongue. Vocal instructors call Romance language vowels "more open." Among the harder languages to pronounce when singing are German, Russian, and English because the consonants, diphthongs, and vowels are harsher.

- Vocal students have at least two and often three parts to their voices: a chest voice, a middle voice, and a head voice. (Actually everybody has these parts to their voices, but only singers care.) They use the chest voice when the notes they sing are in the lower to middle of their range. They use the middle part of the voice to sing in the middle to upper range. They use the head voice when singing in the highest part of their range. Ideally, the movement from one part of the voice to the other (called *passaggio*) should be unnoticeable. Vocal students must work very hard to make that passaggio smooth and connected. Some instructors specialize in the teaching of passaggio. On the other hand, there are teachers who say that there is only one voice and that the student must sing the same way throughout all the registers of the voice.

- Vocal instructors make the students do lots of weird things when teaching them how to breathe. Some teachers make the student lie on the floor in order to feel how the diaphragm naturally expands and contracts when someone is at rest. Others make the student slouch and bend the knees in order to produce a particular sound well. Instructors sometimes ask the student to create strange sounds, which often make a student feel silly. When studying vocal technique, make up your mind to leave your inhibitions at home and do whatever the instructor asks of you, without being embarrassed about it. No matter how weird the exercise is, it has a very logical purpose.

- Once you have found out what the range of your voice is, try not to sing out of that range.
- Make sure the teacher writes all your assignments in a notebook, record all your lessons, and listen to the recordings at home.
- Put your vocalise exercises on a separate recording so that you can practice them at home. Don't practice the vocalises a cappella. Students must train the ear in order to be able to sing on pitch. We call that *intonation*. Practicing with the support of a pitched instrument helps develop that sense. In addition, it's important for the student to stay within his range. If he doesn't know how high or low to go in an exercise, the student might exceed the boundaries of the range.
- Record your practice at home so that you can hear what you actually sound like when you sing. (Warning: It doesn't sound the way you think it does, but the recorder doesn't lie.)
- Many beginning vocal students are surprised to find out that singing requires using parts of the body in different ways than they do in ordinary day-to-day speech.
- Public speakers, orators, actors, and even people in telecommunications often learn vocal techniques in order to make the speaker's voice more resonant or to help preserve and protect the vocal apparatus during long-term use and, in general, to develop the voice to its greatest potential.
- Most instructors agree that beginning vocal students should learn basic vocal technique through classical training, which begins with vocalizing exercises. Vocalises strengthen the vocal cords, extend the range, secure the sound of the voice (which helps it to resonate), teach correct pronunciation of consonants, and place vowels in the proper position for greater clarity.
- The voice is a tool of communication, so it is important that the singer enunciate vowels and consonants so that the listener can understand the words clearly. (If, after he enunciates them clearly

people still can't understand, the singer *might* be singing in a different language—like Martian.)
- Vocal students learn to breathe differently than, say, pianists. Untrained "ordinary" people speak without breathing too deeply. The breath comes from the upper chest and is shallow. Vocal students learn to breathe more deeply and to support and control the breath with the diaphragm. Woodwind and brass players learn to breathe exactly the way singers do. Although we seldom think of it as such, the human voice is actually a wind instrument—the first wind instrument—when used correctly.

Some Basic Tips

Here are some basic tips for learning to sing:

- Open the mouth: the voice is an instrument, and you can't use an instrument if you keep it in the box. The first thing you need to do is to *open the box*. The sound of the voice comes from inside the mouth. The inside of the mouth is like a cavern that enlarges the resonating tube extending from the larynx through the throat, through the mouth, and finally frees the tone.
- The human voice is not just any instrument—it's a wind instrument. Therefore, freedom of the airway is very important in making this wind instrument sound the very best it can. The body parts that sing must conform to the structure, design, and sound of a wind instrument.
- Stand tall (even if you're short). The body must be aligned correctly from the toe to the tip of the head to create a free airway to produce a good sound. The neck should always be relaxed in order to allow free passage of the air as it travels from its lowest level to its highest destination point. The air channel must always be open, free, and clear.
- Breathe low. Feel the breath at the belt level. Lift the ribs, and push the sternum up and out for maximum air capacity.
- Increase throat space. Relax the back of the throat. Yawning helps achieve throat relaxation. The well-produced tone will be rich and ringing, forward yet open. If young singers are learning to sing by listening to the radio or recordings, they may have tightened muscles as a result of imitating untrained high-larynxed gospel or pop singers.
- Pay attention to diction. When a pitch is sung, it is the vowel that is sustained. Consonants stop the sound. However, consonants are very

important if listeners are to understand the words. They also help to bring the tone forward. For example, *fee*, *see*, *wee*, *lee*, and *me* are hard to differentiate unless the consonant is carefully pronounced. Therefore, singers must pay particular attention to the enunciation of each consonant to make it unquestionably clear.

- Sing phrases. Singers have an advantage that other musicians don't have. They have words to help them get across the tone, style, mood, and message of the song. The text and the melody should help the student create logical phrasing. One point to remember: never run out of air in the middle of a phrase, and never, ever breathe in the middle of a word.
- Balance the three registers. Singers must be able to move among the lower, middle, and upper registers of their range with flexibility and ease.
- Singers (like all musicians) must make the musical delivery seem effortless to the listener. Like other musicians, they must practice enough to make vocal technique totally unnoticeable and make the beauty of the voice seem completely natural.

Danger Signs

Vocal students, or anyone who uses the voice a lot, should always be on the lookout for signs of strain:

- sudden changes in pitch while speaking or singing,
- places where the voice cuts out momentarily,
- temporary loss of voice, after yelling or early in the morning,
- hoarseness, breathy or rough sounds,
- frequent sore throats,
- an excessively loud voice,
- the inability to sustain a note while singing, or
- forcing in order to get a note out.

Elements That Cause Strain

Any of the following may contribute to strain:

- contracting the neck or throat muscles when speaking or singing producing squeaky sounds,
- excessive and overly enthusiastic talking for long periods,

- speaking over noise or extraneous sounds or shouting incorrectly,
- beginning a phrase with a sharp glottal attack,
- coughing and loud sneezes,
- clearing the throat to release the discharge associated with postnasal drips,
- dryness in the throat, caused by medication, smoking, or overuse, or
- speaking habitually low in the throat.

Voice is called the most natural instrument. Like other instruments, singing can take many forms and many styles. That doesn't mean it's easy to learn. Like anything else worth mastering, it takes time, effort, and dedication. But for those for whom voice is the instrument of choice, it is the sweetest song.

FOR INSTRUCTORS

Some voice instructors (especially in the United States) don't teach students music notation or theory. They work hard to train the voice itself but leave theory and music notation to other times and other teachers. I recognize that vocal instructors have serious time constraints. Within the teaching hour they must work with the student on a multitude of vocalise exercises. In addition, they must teach phrasing, lyrics, expression, diction, projection, and all the other elements that singing a song requires. That leaves precious little time for notation and theory.

As a result, the majority of vocalists today can sing songs but totally lack other musical skills. That is like learning a speech in Japanese in order to impress a visiting Japanese colleague: the speaker successfully learns the few words he must say but is otherwise totally unable to speak, read, or write the language. Theory is the grammar of the language of music. If a singer knows nothing about this grammar, he will be musically illiterate. A singer? Yes. A musician? No.

Even if teachers of voice spend only a few—perhaps five minutes—of each lesson teaching theory and notation, it will help the student immeasurably.

Over the years, many vocal students have told me that they had voice lessons in the past but never learned anything about theory or notation. As a result, they never felt that they really understood the how, what, and whys of music. Oh, they understood the workings of the voice box, but music? Well, that they never learned.

As I said earlier, just playing the instrument (in this case, singing) is only part of the story. An engineer, a doctor, a dentist, a lawyer—they don't learn part of the story. They learn the whole story. Of course they may specialize in one area of their profession or another, but long before they get to that stage they learned the basics. In music, theory is as basic as it gets.

In a sense, we have come full circle. I spoke in the beginning of this book of a need to make sure students understand everything they possibly can about music in order to get the greatest benefit from their instruction. I said it then, and it bears repeating: students must know not only what to do but why to do it and how it relates to the big picture. Music students aren't just pianists, cellists, flute players, or singers who play their instruments or sing in a vacuum. They should be complete musicians. Therefore, it is very important that students learn all the ramifications of the language of music so that they can become musicians in the fullest sense of the word. It is the duty and privilege of instructors everywhere to help our students reach that goal.

16

MENTE SANA IN CORPO SANO

Music Instruction as an Aid in Physical and Emotional Therapy

Music was my refuge. I could crawl into the space between the notes and curl my back to loneliness.

—Maya Angelou, writer

PRELUDE

The young man said to the instructor, "I've always wanted to study guitar, but I never had the time until now. My whole life I've loved this instrument so much. The sound of the guitar is so passionate, so exquisite. The sound of the guitar has haunted me all my life. Whenever I heard it I cried. When I was a child I asked my parents for lessons, but they couldn't afford it. And after I began working I had so little free time. I didn't want to start because I knew I didn't have time to practice. Now I have plenty of time."

The instructor looked at him and smiled gently. "Isn't it strange how things work out?"

The young man sat up straighter in the seat and asked, "Well, what do you think? Can you help me? Do you think I can really learn to play this beautiful thing?" He ran his right hand over the wood of the instrument, caressing it.

The instructor replied with a smile, "I think we can give it a good shot. Of course, before we start lessons we'll have to restring the guitar in the opposite direction."

"Why?" asked the young man, perplexed.

"Because you're going to have to learn to play the fingerboard with your right hand instead of your left and to pick with your left. Ordinarily people do the fingerboard with the left hand and pick with the right. We'll have to restring the guitar in the opposite direction so that you can play it. Don't worry. We can do it easily. It'll be fine."

The young man bent over, gently put the guitar into its case, and locked it. He petted the closed case one more time and sat up straight. "My doctor was sure that you could help. That's why he sent me here. He wants me to learn to use this . . . this . . . this *thing* quickly so that I can go back to living my life. Man, it's so heavy; it weighs a ton. Anyhow, the doctor thought that guitar lessons would help speed things up."

The instructor smiled. "Your doctor is right. You'll see. When you can use it to play the guitar, it won't feel heavy at all." The instructor continued, with a little chuckle, "And think of how much money you'll save in picks! I'll see you next week, Thursday at 4 P.M. Bring the guitar, and we'll restring it then."

"Thank you so much," said the man. "You really have put me at ease. I feel so much better already. I've been so upset since the car accident. You have no idea. I wanted to die. I can't go back to work like this. I just can't."

"Let's tackle one thing at a time. For now, let's just think about learning to play this instrument you've wanted so long. Isn't it nice that now you have time? But you must promise you'll practice every day."

The young man stood up. He chuckled with a certain irony in his voice. "Yeah, well, you're right. Now there's nothing but time." He took his jacket from the chair and started to put it on.

The instructor stood up, also. "Good. Then I'll see you next week, Thursday, 4 P.M. Here—let me help you with your jacket."

"Thank you. That's kind of you. I guess I do need a lot of help."

"Don't worry about it. Soon you'll be just fine. You'll see."

The instructor held the jacket for the young man. He put his left arm into the sleeve. The hook from the prosthesis caught in the lining.

FOR EVERYONE

In the beginning of this book I said that, generally speaking, there are three reasons that students study music: some want to take up music as a hobby, some want careers in music, and some want music for its therapeutic benefits. This chapter is geared specifically toward folks who would benefit from music as therapy.

The Role of Music in Everyday Life

Music plays a large role in our lives. It very often dictates what we feel and what we think. For more than a hundred years the film industry has used music to prepare moviegoers emotionally for what is to come in the story. Indeed, the music during the opening credits tells us whether the film will be funny, sad, frightening, or romantic. Who can forget the theme from *Jaws* that warned us that whatever was swimming toward us in the water was something we didn't want to meet close up?

Music has been used as a tranquilizer in biorhythm adjustments, as an aid in meditation, as a companion when driving, as a stimulant for studying, and even as an accompaniment for shopping. And what about soft lights and romantic music to set a mood in a fine restaurant?

Music Therapy

Music has been shown to be a very effective tool in physical and emotional therapy: it can raise and lower blood pressure and the heart rate, lower levels of stress, stimulate brain waves, increase concentration and alertness, ease muscle tension, and help with pain management. For those reasons, as well as a multitude of other healing benefits, the music-therapy profession has become a very important part of the health-care industry. Treatment may include listening to music, reacting to music, singing, movement, song writing, lyric analysis, improvisation, and actually making music by playing instruments. Percussion instruments that require little or no instruction are popular in music therapy, as are piano, violin, guitar, and flute. Although the patient may, indeed, receive music instruction, therapy is the main thrust of the activity. The goal is to address and alleviate a problem through the treatment.

MiPet Program

There is another field just beginning to emerge: Music Instruction as an aid in Physical and Emotional Therapy (MiPet). The MiPet program is somewhat different from music therapy. In Music Instruction as an aid in Physical and Emotional Therapy the instruction is the focus; the person receiving the instruction is considered a student rather than a patient, and the instruction is used as an adjunct to whatever other therapy is being administered. The supervising health-care professional, the instructor, and the student make decisions regarding the best choice of instrument, curricula are developed, and instruments may need to be modified as necessary. The goal is for the student to learn to play the instrument or sing to the extent to which he is capable, and a byproduct of the instruction is, hopefully, alleviation of the original problem. The student in a MiPet program is expected to practice at home daily, and his progress is carefully monitored by the instructor as it would be with any healthy student.

Stutterers Don't Stutter When They Sing

Did you know that stutterers don't stutter when they sing? As I said in the previous chapter, good vocal instructors teach students how to care for and protect the voice. Therefore, a vocal student's technique training includes control of the vocal cords, tongue, palate, mouth, lips, teeth, jaw, facial and chest muscles, lungs, and diaphragm. Vocal students learn proper breathing, focus and projection of sound, placement of voice, enunciation, pitch clarity, intonation, and the speed and rhythm of syllables. This fine tuning and control of the voice helps diminish and may eliminate stuttering (or stammering) in speech.

Asthmatics and Emphysema

Asthmatics in otherwise good medical condition and emphysema patients may also benefit from proper vocal instruction, because they are taught to breathe uniformly from the diaphragm, relax the muscles, and keep the airways open, making better use of their lung capacity. Determining that an asthmatic is in otherwise good medical condition may sound like an oxymoron, but it isn't. What it means is that other than the asthmatic condition, they are physically healthy. Practicing a reed instrument like saxophone may also be helpful to asthmatics in good medical condition.

Damaged Voices

Public speakers, salespersons, telemarketers, teachers, and others who speak professionally a great deal often suffer from laryngitis or sore throats caused by overuse of the voice. In a nontrained voice, the muscles that suspend the larynx strain against each other. Good vocal training can get these muscles to work together.[1] Vocal motor skills lost or diminished after illness or surgery may also benefit from singing instruction.

Arthritis and Stiffness

Arthritis pain and stiffness in the fingers and hands can be alleviated by playing an electronic keyboard (usually not the piano). It takes much less pressure and motion to play an electronic key than a piano key. The gentle exercise involved in playing the keyboard keeps the fingers moving and loosens the muscles, joints, and tendons. Moving hurts but doesn't destroy. Incorrect moving harms, but correct moving heals.[2]

Manual Prostheses

Patients with a manual prosthesis can enhance their fine motor skills by learning the guitar, mandolin, lute, ukulele, bass, banjo, or other similar nonbowed instruments. Instructors teach the student to pick or strum the instrument with the prosthesis and play the fingerboard with the good hand. (In order to learn the instrument this way, it is often necessary to reverse the strings.) Using the prosthesis to strum while playing an instrument enables the student to quickly learn to use the prosthesis with a minimum of frustration because the student enjoys playing the instrument.

Hearing Disorders

Music lessons on a fixed-pitch keyboard instrument (piano, organ, xylophone, vibraphone, or marimba) may help to alleviate a mild hearing problem by training the ear to identify differences in sound—including pitch, volume, ranges, timbre, and resonance.

Memory Problems

Because playing a musical instrument is a learned automatic movement (remember LAM?), students with memory problems benefit from music instruction. The many repetitions, the attention to detail, and the general complexities of practice stimulate and develop certain kinds of memory: kinesthetic (which keys the fingers hit and what movements the hand must make), aural (sound of the music), visual (the music the student reads), and rhythmic (the pulse).

Learning Disabilities

Developing concentration is especially important for students with learning disabilities. Music students learn not to play through a piece but to rather practice small passages and make many repetitions. The ability to focus on a small part and repeat it many times makes it easier for a learning-challenged person to absorb the information. In addition, this capacity to focus sometimes becomes the means for shutting out the cares of the day, a particular plus for people with difficult jobs or those who are otherwise frequently in emotionally stressful situations.

Coordination

Coordination, another major problem in students with learning problems, often improves with music training because of the simultaneous use of eyes, ears, mouth, fingers, hands, and brain in much repeated exercises. Left-right discrimination, perception, and understanding of basic mathematical concepts are also developed, as is multilevel thinking.

ADHD Children and Adults

The hyperactivity, irritability, difficulty in focusing, and disruptive behavior suffered by many ADHD children and adults often dramatically improve through music instruction that challenges the student and captures the imagination. Many students with behavioral problems also respond positively to music training. Good music instruction teaches self-discipline, problem solving, goal setting, perseverance, and the patience to see a project to its conclusion. And, of course, the complexities of studying music stimulate the creative side of the brain.

Many parents believe that because a child suffers from ADHD he can't sit through or focus during a lesson, much less do systematic daily practice. Research shows that the opposite is true. Little by little good music instruction gradually helps a student to develop the ability to concentrate and focus.

Lack of Confidence and Self-Esteem

Many people suffer from a lack of confidence and low self-esteem. Music instruction affords an opportunity for many small successes. Students progress from "No, I can't" to "Wow—yes, I can!" With each small success the feeling of pride and accomplishment increases.

Other Conditions

Music Instruction as an aid in Physical and Emotional Therapy may also help alleviate some forms of autism, certain kinds of palsy, depression, and problems with breathing, speech, and aggression. MiPet focuses on positive attitudes and helps to lessen stress levels and promote a sense of well-being. While music instruction will not give a blind person sight and won't make a deaf person hear, it may diminish many conditions and often helps improve mental, physical, and emotional health.

FOR PARENTS

Parents whose children suffer from various illnesses or conditions that they believe may be alleviated through a MiPet or music-therapy program should discuss this option with the doctors or the health-care professionals overseeing the child's care. Of course, the MiPet program only works if the child particularly likes music and would enjoy learning to play a musical instrument.

Before embarking on such a plan of treatment it is important that the student be thoroughly evaluated through a complete physical and emotional workup. In addition, a music-aptitude test should be administered that is specifically designed to determine the most appropriate instrument, course of study, need for modification of the instrument or parts of the instrument, and anticipated degree of improvement. This evaluation should be jointly assessed and discussed by the attending medical practitioner, the music professional, and the parent.

Physicians and other medical professionals considering music instruction as an aid in therapy should discuss the specific needs of the patient and the potential for success with the music instructor, and the instructor should be fully and openly apprised of the student's condition. During the course of the lessons the instructor should have ongoing access to and discussions with those in charge of the case to discuss the student's progress, and there should be periodic reevaluations to determine the program's efficacy.

FOR STUDENTS

Sometimes older persons, adults, and senior citizens enjoy music and would like to learn to play a musical instrument or sing but think that they are hampered by some preexisting illness or condition. These folks should discuss their concerns with their health-care professional. The physician or health-care professional in charge of the case may feel that music instruction would be helpful in improving, alleviating, or managing the preexisting problem. As an example, many older adults are not as active, interested, involved, or alert as they could be. While they might not be physically ill, some develop an apathy that is difficult to penetrate. They may suffer from a multitude of complaints, some of them real, some perceived. Learning music can bring interest and purpose back to their lives. It can change the way they act, the way they feel, and their general outlook, not just about themselves but about the outside world as well. It can even find for them their heretofore forgotten joy of living.

Anyone contemplating music instruction for therapy should first have a complete physical and emotional workup and thoroughly discuss the ramifications of taking lessons with their health-care provider and a music instructor who is specifically trained to offer music instruction as an aid in physical and emotional therapy.

FOR INSTRUCTORS

Music therapy has been a respected part of the health-care industry for many years. The subject of Music Instruction as an aid in Physical and Emotional Therapy, on the other hand, is very new, and although some instructors have been using it as a part of their teaching practice for years, it is only now beginning to gain recognition. Music instructors who wish to teach the MiPet program require special training apart from music therapy. Although parts of the two disciplines converge, the MiPet program takes students who want to learn to play a musical instrument or sing for its therapeutic benefits in a different direction and offers them a goal other than that provided by music therapy.

NOTES

Much of the information in this chapter was originally published in *Miami Medicine*, the Dade County Medical Association journal (June 1995: 31–32) in Phyllis Sdoia-Satz's article "Music Instruction as an Aid to Physical and Emotional Therapy."

1. According to Laurence Levine, M.D., of Washington University School of Medicine in St. Louis, Missouri.
2. According to Mary P. Schatz, M.D., of Nashville, Tennessee.

EPILOGO: PRACTICING SUCKS, BUT IT DOESN'T HAVE TO!

After reading all the information in this little book, if you are still considering beginning music lessons, good for you! That means you *really* want to do it and that you are at least minimally ready to face the many valleys that will follow the exciting peaks from the start of your lessons until that time when you finally achieve your goals. If this book has given you a lot to think about and once or twice has caused you to say to yourself, "Wow, I didn't know that, but it makes sense," then it has done its job.

Remember in the beginning when we said that the majority of people approach music lessons with no clue about how long it will take or how hard they will have to work. If they did, most of them wouldn't even start. There is no question that learning to play a musical instrument or sing is not all fun and games. Every professional musician recognizes that it is hard work—and lots of it. The purpose of this book has been to offer some tips to help students learn faster, easier, with less stress and more success. If you follow at least some of the suggestions in this book you will avoid some of the problems, make some of the difficulties easier, and, best of all, make the enjoyment come sooner.

Now that you have just about finished this book, read it again. Make some notes for yourself. They will help you get started. Although everything in this book is important, not everything is necessarily immediately applicable. Some things will be very helpful even before you begin instruction, while others will become clear only after you've had a few lessons; still others will be really applicable after you've been studying a few months. Therefore, keep going back to the book. Use the table of contents like a book of recipes.

Let's review a few of the basics:

Look for the best instructor you can find. Ask lots of questions. Make a list of things you want to know, and use that for reference. Don't let anyone intimidate you. It's your money, your time, and your effort.

Find a good student instrument without spending a fortune, and make sure it is in good repair. Nothing frustrates a student more than playing on an instrument that doesn't work right.

Make sure the instrument fits the person. Stringed instruments should be sized for the student. Woodwind and brass instruments should be started later than stringed instruments because the student requires more lung capacity to blow them. Pianos should be full-size, with eighty-eight keys, weighted, and velocity sensitive, with at least two pedals. Although there are many electronic keyboards with only sixty-one keys (and some with even less), it is best to have a full-size, eighty-eight-note keyboard. Anything less will limit how and what the student can learn.

Here's an important point that I didn't mention earlier: Try very hard to obtain your own instrument. How often teachers have heard, "My cousin has a piano at her house, and she lives only ten minutes from me. I can practice there"; or "there's an organ at my church, and the pastor has said that I can practice there anytime I want." That may work in the short term, but typically not on a long-term, every-day basis. Church staff sometimes lock their buildings, and students can't get in to practice. Cousins may be unavailable at the time the student wants to practice. If a student likes to practice more than one time in a day (maybe twenty minutes early, twenty minutes later, and thirty-five minutes even later), she can't do that if the instrument is at a different location or belongs to someone else. In addition, if the instrument needs repair, it can be awkward for the student to say to the owner of the instrument, "Listen, your cello has a broken bridge. You need to get it fixed." The answer to that would be "Why? You're the only one who uses it." Not good. Really, really not good. It's much better to have your own instrument and be able to go to it at seven o'clock in the morning or eleven o'clock at night and not be dependent on someone else. If you can't buy your own instrument, rent it.

Always get the materials the teacher tells you to get in a timely manner. "I was too busy," "I forgot," or "I was out of town" won't cut it. The longer it takes to get the material, the more frustration builds up.

Never look at a clock when you are learning music. Just practice. Keep your mind focused on what you are working on. Don't think of what you have to do later. The more you concentrate on practicing, the sooner you will learn it. If you get really tired, stop, and go back to it later. (This doesn't mean work five minutes and quit.) There's absolutely no rule that says you must practice all in one session each day. Stop whenever you like, and go back to it later. Just make sure you actually go back to it.

Never decide that you are going to practice for a particular amount of time. When a student does that, she's concentrating on quantity, not quality. Better to practice less but make it productive.

Practice every day—not just most days, but every day! Productive practice means daily repetitions. The brain and the body require a certain number of repetitions to learn any particular section of music. That number is generally in the hundreds and sometimes in the thousands. The fewer the repetitions or the more days there are between practices, the longer it takes to really know the part. The more repetitions you make, and the more times you do it every day, especially in the first few weeks, the sooner the hands and the brain learn it. You do the math and tell me which is more effective.

Don't pick and choose which parts of the lesson or parts of the instructions to do and which to ignore. Music instruction is not a smorgasbord. If you trust the instructor's teaching skills, then do what you have been assigned—not some of it, all of it! If you don't trust the teacher's teaching skills, then find another teacher.

If there is anything you don't understand, call the instructor. Ask for clarification. Make sure you understand the instructions and explanations and then do it; practice according to those instructions.

If the instructor tells you to practice only one hand, don't practice with two hands. If the instructor tells you to practice with two hands, don't practice with one.

And never, never go ahead of the instructor. There's a good chance you'll learn incorrectly or introduce bad habits if you haven't first worked on a passage with your instructor. Therefore, always wait for the instructor to introduce and work through a new section with you before going home to practice it on your own.

Never practice by playing through a piece, no matter how short it seems or how easy you think it's going to be. If you were to learn a foreign language, the shortest, simplest sentence would be very hard to learn but would be easier if you were to break it up into smaller parts. Studying music is very much the same thing. There is a lot to think about in every phrase of music. Working in very small sections (not more than one or two measures at a time) and making lots of repetitions until you learn them may seem silly and like a waste of time. On the contrary, it is much more productive than trying to learn a relatively long passage by playing it through in its entirety.

Don't just play blind, thoughtless repetitions. Know what you are working for, and check yourself after each repetition to make sure you are accomplishing your goal.

Make sure you're always counting when you practice. Rhythm is equally, if not more important than, notes. Don't try to learn the notes first and then the rhythm, because it won't work. Learn both at the same time.

Watch the music, not the hands, and learn to read the notes as quickly as you can. Learning to read the music is as important for musicians as is learning to read books for students in school. A musician who learns to play without reading the music is like the actor who learns his part by rote but can't read the script. Learning by rote or by ear is only part of the story, and what you should be aiming for is the whole story.

Music notation is part of music theory. Theory is the grammar of music, the mechanics of why we do what we do. As such, theory is necessary, even crucial, to learning and understanding music. Use flashcards, theory games, exercises, props in music stores, and anything you can find, but learn theory and music notation. That goes for vocalists as well as instrumentalists.

You will get frustrated. A lot. Be prepared for it. And be prepared to practice in spite of it and, in some cases, right through it. Sometimes the worst moments happen just before we learn a section once and for all. It's like a battle: sometimes the fingers fight hardest just before they surrender. If you keep practicing the piece, there comes a moment when all the cobwebs are brushed away and everything is right. And when that happens, when we play it and we realize that, "Wow, yes! Yes, yes, yes, I can!" that's when the study of music becomes not just fun but utter, complete enjoyment with a wonderful sense of accomplishment.

There may be periodic frustrations after that, because what you've gained could be accidental, or you could make some mistakes in the next play-through. However, having once been able to perform the passage correctly, real triumph is just a hair's breadth away—maybe a week or so of additional practice before you experience the joy of winning not just one battle but the whole war. And with victory comes the fun—playing the piece for others and having them ooh, ah, and applaud, knowing in your heart that you can play this piece anytime you want, anywhere you want and it will always be good. You've learned it. You've earned your right to the piece—maybe by blood, sweat, and tears, but it's yours, nonetheless. It belongs to you.

There's a special trick here: once you've learned a piece, you have to keep doing it, because after a little while if you don't play it, your hand, your mind, and your body will forget how, and you'll have to learn it all over again. And you really don't want to do that, do you?

Therefore, always review what you have already learned so as not to forget. Too many students spend a lot of time learning something and then, because they never play it again, forget it within a few weeks of having finished it. The pleasure of learning music is in being able to execute it. Therefore, a few times a week sit down at the instrument and play through the pieces you already know. Play them for anybody, even the guppy in the fish tank, but play them—for fun, for relaxation, for you! Little by little, develop a repertoire of pieces that you can play anytime, anywhere, for anyone. You'll be surprised how fast the repertoire grows.

Remember to learn and to memorize using many kinds of techniques—LAM, thought memory, analysis, saying notes, playing music in your head, and even thinking about it before going to sleep (gives a whole new meaning to *sleeping on it*, doesn't it?).

To ease boredom, practice with different rhythms, different articulations, different tempos, different registers—anything except different fingerings. Always practice with the same fingerings so that the fingers learn the motions.

Remember that SACs are part of the foundation of learning music. They are important for students at all stages of their instruction. Practice them diligently, even if you think they're annoying. They will help your technique and help you develop evenness and uniformity. They will help every aspect of your playing or singing.

Most importantly, practice as much as you can, whenever you can. Even when there seems to be no improvement, practice. Even when you are really, really tired after a long day, practice. When you feel frustrated, isolated, and like you are getting nowhere, practice. Even when your progress seems to be slipping away, practice. Every time you push yourself to practice past that frustration point, you make it easier for your brain and your body to learn.

Playing music or singing for a hobby is not something that has a limited time frame. The pleasure of music is for a lifetime. Over the years, many students have said to me, "Gee, I wish I hadn't stopped taking lessons; I'd be so good by now." And I tell them that no one is too old to learn, and no one is too young to begin. So, tell me, why are you still sitting there? Go find a teacher. The joy of learning music is waiting for you.

Not the end; only the beginning . . .

GLOSSARY

A cappella	Without musical accompaniment. Usually used for singers. Like when you sing in the shower. Most folks don't have an orchestra in the shower with them. So they sing a cappella.
Accelerando	Put the pedal to the metal
Allegretto	*Allegro* means *fast*, and *-etto* means *a little bit*, so basically *allegretto* means *a little bit fast*, only it doesn't. *Allegretto* actually means a speed that's a little bit cutesy-pie, a little flirty, a little playful.
Allegro	Fast. Yes, I know, in Spanish it means *happy*, but this is Italian, and it means *fast*.
Allegro assai	Pretty fast, or quite fast, or fast enough, or, well, you get the idea, don't you?
Al perfezione	This is Italian for *perfection*. It's the same as the Latin *perfection*, only more emotional.
Alto	A low lady's voice or a medium-voiced instrument. If that's not clear, see *tenor*.
Baritone horn	A horn with a deep sound
Bar lines	Vertical lines that separate measures of music
Bass	Not a fish. It's the big, tall instrument that looks like a violin with a really, really bad case of mumps.

Cantando espressivo	No, it's not a coffee drink. *Cantando* means *singing*, and *espressivo* means *expressively*; so *cantando espressivo* means *singing your guts out*.
Chord	A bunch of notes played together, or a bunch of grapes, or a bunch of broccoli
Clarinet	A woodwind instrument with a rich, sexy sound
Clef	A musical sign. It can mean to play high up or low down or someplace you didn't expect to have to play.
Con moto	Translated freely, it means *whatever parts of you that you need to rev up to do something, rev 'em up, and get it done.*
Crescendo	Gradually getting louder, and louder, and louder, and louder
Cymbalom	A musical stringed instrument on four legs, shaped like a trapezoid (if you don't know what that is, go ask a math teacher, not a music teacher), or a rectangle with horizontal strings. The player makes musical sounds by hitting the strings with felted hammers, which he holds like drumsticks in his hands. The ends of the sticks look like the shoes that elves wear. The cymbalom sounds like a cross between a piano and a harp.
Delicatissimo	What do you think it means? I'll give you a hint: *-issimo* means *very*.
Diaphragm	The part of the body that helps expand the lungs and . . . Oh, go ask a doctor. Anyhow, vocal students talk about the importance of diaphragms a lot. It's sort of their thing.
Diminuendo	Gradually getting softer and softer and softer
Ensembles	The family that plays together stays together. Well, maybe not always.
Epilogo	Hmm, if *prologo* is *the beginning*, then *epilogo* must mean . . . maybe *the middle*?
Falsetto	Where a male sings in a high register that isn't naturally part of his vocal range. When a guy sings like a girl, that's falsetto, meaning *not his natural voice*. It's a "false" voice.
French Horn	A horn with a passport and a work permit
Gradus ad parnassus	It's Latin (how did Latin get in here?) for *steps to perfection*. But actually I borrowed the term from Claude Debussy, who was French.

Inversion	If you turn over a cup, it's inverted. ·If you turn over a chord, you put the bottom note on top or the middle note on top or the top note on bottom or the middle note on the . . . Are you *trying* to make me crazy?
Key signature	Tells what key we are playing by showing sharps and flats . . . Oh, you don't know what they are either, so forget I said anything.
Lento	No, it's not a religious holiday; it means *slowly*.
L'istesso tempo	*Tempo* means *time* or *speed*. *L'istesso* means *the same*. So *l'istesso tempo* means *the same speed* or *keep the same speed*; but it really doesn't matter what it means, because everyone thinks of it as *the first speed*, the speed one uses in the beginning of a piece. But don't worry about it, because even musicians get this term wrong. So forget I even said anything.
Measure	The music written in between vertical lines. No, we're not talking about jail, and you can't get a drink there. It's just the way music is written.
Misterioso	Get the toddlers out of here; it could get scary.
Molto appassionato	Very intense, very passionate, very . . . You get the picture, right?
Oboe	A woodwind instrument. Sounds a lot like a clarinet with a cold.
Ocarina	A very, very old flute-like instrument. Looks like an egg with a lot of holes in it. It also sounds like an egg with a lot of holes in it.
Poco agitato	A little agitated. Now you know what *agitated* means, don't you? It's a little upset, and annoyed, and irritated, and angry, and someone who is *poco agitato* isn't a happy camper.
Prologo	It's a prologue; what did you think it was, a chicken?
Recorder	No, it's not an electronic gadget; it's the grandfather of a flute. Looks sort of like a clarinet knockoff. Sounds like a . . . Never mind, you won't like it.
Register	The area where the sound is (or where the money is). Bears growl in a low register. Birds tweet in a high register. Male singers sing in a low register, females in a high or middle register.

Repertoire	A whole bunch of music you learned when you were ten years old that we hope you can still play when you're fifty
Risoluto	Resolute, determined, stoic-faced and -minded. The music probably sounds like someone who's very determined and very disciplined and very boring.
Ritardando	Gradually getting slower. If you put together *ritardando* and *accelerando* and *crescendo* and *diminuendo*, you can confuse the person playing to no end. He'll be getting louder and softer and faster and slower all at the same time, and before you know it he'll be meeting himself coming and going.
Ritorno vincitor	Translated freely, it means *if you're going to come back a loser, don't bother coming back at all.*
Soprano	Hmm. A high lady's voice or a high-sounding instrument. If that's not clear, see *alto.*
Tenor	A high man's voice. If that's not clear see *bass.* Definitely do not go to *soprano.* Sopranos and tenors do not mix well and usually end in some terrible operatic finale where everybody dies.
Tin whistle	A woodwind instrument. Wikipedia describes it as a "fipple flute." Need I say more?
Toccata	From the Italian word *toccare*, which means *to touch*, and I'm not even gonna go there.
Triad	A chord of three notes, *tri* is the same as *bi* or *di*, only three.
Triplets	No, not that kind of triplets. Musical triplets are groups of three notes where there usually are only one or two notes. Sort of the same as triplet children, only they're notes.
Tuba	Largest of the brass instruments. It's so big that a small person could live in it for a month before realizing that it doesn't have a bathroom.
Vibrato	It's a natural trembling sound that a singing voice makes that creates a very warm, resonant tone.
Vocalises	Vocal exercises that are meant to stretch and strengthen the vocal cords and muscles, but what they really do is stretch the patience of any family members listening. Sounds a lot like a cat screeching.

ABOUT THE AUTHORS

Phyllis Sdoia-Satz, educator, pianist, composer, and author is the product of a musical family. She began piano lessons at the age of two and a half. At five, she got her first "professional gig" playing piano in the window of Steinway and Sons in New York City on weekends. In her youth, she won countless national and international competitions and numerous other awards. She has appeared in solo recitals on the concert stage, on TV and radio, and has been guest artist with many of the world's finest orchestras. She graduated from the "Fame" school (LaGuardia High School of Music and Art and the Performing Arts) and at sixteen, played a New York debut. She holds a bachelor's degree with highest honors from Florida International University and did her graduate work with distinction at the University of Miami. Her articles, books, teaching methods, and innovative views on music education have appeared in many publications. Her article, "Music Instruction as an Aid to Physical and Emotional Therapy" was even featured in a medical journal. Her textbook, *The Art of Teaching Music: A Basic Text* is a "must-read" for both experienced teachers and those just starting out in the field of education. She conducts seminars, workshops, and master classes worldwide which are widely attended by both lay people and professionals, and appears often on TV news programs and talk shows.

Ms. Sdoia-Satz has been teaching for many years and writing music and stories since childhood. Among her many musical compositions are works for piano and other solo instruments, as well as larger works for full orchestra and chorus, including several tone poems, and a cantata for four soloists, chorus, and orchestra. Ms. Sdoia-Satz is the founder and executive director of Sdoia-Satz Music Institute (The Husky Gang School) in Miami, Florida. She is the author/composer of the first three books in *The Husky Gang Teaches . . .* series of adventure stories, educational books, and CDs, (Warner Bros. 2001), and *Husky Gang Tales* (Warner Bros. 2002). All four Husky Gang Books, CDs, and flash cards are now in their third printing. Her most recent work: *The Life and Times of Sasha, The Sad Ferret*, an illustrated children's story for piano and narrator has recently been made into a CD and DVD and will be in stores soon. For further information, please see sdoiasatz.com or musicschool.cc.

Barry Satz and Phyllis Sdoia-Satz have been married for fifty-two years. They have four children, eleven grandchildren, and three great-grandchildren. Although Barry and Phyllis were born in New York City, they now reside in Miami. Over the years, Mr. Satz has had several careers and worn many hats. He holds a master's degree in engineering and was a professional engineer for more than forty years. In addition, Mr. Satz was a decorated New York City reserve police officer for twenty years. He is co-author of *Husky Gang Tales* and *Practicing Sucks!!!*, as well as administrator of the Sdoia-Satz Music Institute. Most importantly, he is the inspiration for everything that Ms. Sdoia-Satz does.